When Spelling Matters

Developing writers who
can spell and understand
language

Doreen Scott-Dunne

Pembroke Publishers Limited

Dedicated to husband, Ray Scanlan,
who has given me unconditional love and constant encouragement,
and who never ceases to believe in me

© 2013 Pembroke Publishers
538 Hood Road
Markham, Ontario, Canada L3R 3K9
www.pembrokepublishers.com

Distributed in the U.S. by Stenhouse Publishers
480 Congress Street
Portland, ME 04101
www.stenhouse.com

We acknowledge the financial support of the Government of Canada through the
Canada Book Fund (CBF) for our publishing activities.

We acknowledge the assistance of the Government of Ontario through the Ontario
Media Development Corporation's Ontario Book Initiative.

Library and Archives Canada Cataloguing in Publication

Scott-Dunne, Doreen
    When spelling matters : developing writers who can spell and understand language /
Doreen Scott-Dunne.

Includes bibliographical references and index. Issued also in electronic format.
ISBN 978-1-55138-277-7

1. English language — Orthography and spelling — Study and teaching (Elementary).
I. Title.

LB1574.S36 2012   372.63'2044   C2012-903953-5

---

eBook format ISBN 978-1-55138-844-1

Editor: Kate Revington
Cover Design: John Zehethofer
Typesetting: Jay Tee Graphics Ltd.

Printed and bound in Canada
9 8 7 6 5 4 3 2 1

Contents

Introduction: Why Spelling Matters

As a classroom teacher, I used to send a note home asking students to bring in typical writing samples — lists, informal notes, reminders, letters, instructions, directions, recipes, anything their parents would approve of them bringing. Then I made a bulletin board of a variety of texts. I had told parents that these writing samples would be displayed, and they were quite relaxed about it. However, when parents came to class and saw their lists or notes there, a few were motivated to edit and correct spelling, even to improve the note paper, because their writing was on public display in the classroom. Several parents requested that I return certain pieces to them and then replaced them with perfectly edited work. At the time, I used this experience to illustrate to students that a note or list is informal, but once writing goes on display, usually spelling matters.

Spelling does *not* matter when you are celebrating the first attempts of Grade 1 writers to create text, however. Their work is worthy of display, even if it is not perfect. If displayed in a hallway for parents to see, though, I suggest that it be edited, with the original copy beside it. We need to remember that our goal is to achieve fluency with young writers; nevertheless, we also want to teach students multiple word patterns and see their knowledge of how words work growing daily. As a student's knowledge grows as a writer and as a worker with words, so will the student's confidence grow as a speller.

The Need for Clear Communication and Positive Impressions

Spelling matters when there is a need for clear communication because both writer and reader have to understand what is being said. Misspelling can sometimes interfere, like an annoying distraction, as the reader struggles to interpret the misspelled words.

Spelling matters when work is published at the end of the writing process and when work will be shared publicly for others to read. That sharing could include blogs because, while like a journal in some respects, blogs have a wider audience. Checking spelling on a blog would be a personal decision related to the impression that the writer wants to make. Spelling matters when text is in final draft, to be assessed by the teacher.

Spelling matters when formal letters are written because multiple misspellings can create a bad impression of the writer to the reader. Teachers will know that accurate spelling is particularly important on a job application, on a resumé, or in an article to be published in the school newsletter.

Spelling matters in a reference context when, for example, the student is composing a word list, copying a word pattern, or preparing a personal dictionary.

Spelling matters when a book is published, either as a commercial novel or as a short story for a class anthology. It also matters when a report or other text form is completed, ready to be submitted to the teacher for final marking.

Spelling really matters when teachers are writing report cards, as these records are being read by the principal, students, and parents. Teachers need to model good spelling!

Spelling is very much about appearances if the writing is a public piece.

A Focus on Getting Out the Thoughts

Spelling does not matter when students are writing responses to a book they have read. The thinking is what matters then — not the spelling.

Spelling does not matter in first- or second-draft writing because the focus is on composing, not on mechanics.

Spelling does not matter in journal writing because the writing is informal, not public. Indeed, spelling does not matter in any kind of informal writing, as long as it does not interfere with meaning. So, if a student writes, "come to my howse tonight" to a friend, the friend will understand the message.

Spelling does not matter when texting a friend, either, although rereading text is important — when texting, the spellchecker may create a word that was unintended by the writer and which changes the meaning. However, if texting is someone's major means of communication, then it's important to remember how words are *really* spelled for more formal writing.

On the home front, spelling does not matter when listing groceries to buy or jobs to be done. Only the author needs to understand the content.

A Long Way from "I Have a Cat"

So, spelling does not matter all the time, but it does matter some of the time. For teachers, then, it is important to identify the occasions when they should expect accurate spelling and to recognize the best contexts for enabling students to learn to spell correctly.

We have already come a long way from students writing "I have a cat" when they did not even have a pet but could spell the words *have* and *cat*. Now we might have a young student writing, "The big idea in this book is betrayal," referring to a book that the teacher had read aloud. Note that if this is a reading response and *betrayal* is misspelled, it is more important for the student to identify the big idea, through synthesis, than to spell *betrayal* correctly. As time goes on, and knowledge of words increases, the student will spell the word correctly, too.

The key premise of this book is that children learn to spell by investigating how words work and by building spelling patterns for themselves. These inquiries into language will help students to understand how words work in the context of spelling and how words fit into different patterns, which they can access when they write. They should then be able to apply their growing word knowledge directly to editing their writing, as application is key to their success. Lessons that take the developmental nature of spelling into account and can be taught explicitly are outlined here.

When Spelling Matters also provides teachers with ways to help their students deal with the hard task of editing. Students need to be able to edit their work for specific items, such as checking for the 50 most common words, for endings, or for plurals. They also need to check whether they have used the correct homonym, since *there* and *their*, for example, are more often misused than misspelled. When students learn the word *there* in the context of "somewhere, anywhere, and everywhere," and the word *their* in the context of "my, his, her, and our," then perhaps they will remember to use the correct word in context, and thus spell it correctly.

Spelling as Manifesting a Love of Words

The problem with formal spelling instruction is the lack of transfer from rote memorization of words to application of this knowledge in writing and editing. Spelling application is enabled by problem solving with words, working out their structure, and perceiving how they fit into patterns. This understanding reflects that spelling is not a low-level, rote-memory activity, but a high-level cognitive skill.

A viable solution for the teaching of spelling in today's classroom is to have students develop a love of words — indeed, to create students who are wordsmiths, lovers of metaphors and word origins. Students can come to see language as a valuable resource to be explored deeply. My experience has shown that once students gain this perspective, they are more likely to have something to say when they write and will produce pieces of writing worth editing and reading.

In summary, here is what matters to helping your students become proficient spellers:

- opportunities for inquiry into word patterns
- a growing developmental knowledge of word structure
- opportunities to write and think and solve word problems

Thinking always matters because learning to spell always involves *thinking about words* while *working with words*. Spelling is not some cosmetic device but a way in which to help writers communicate with purpose and clarity.

1

In the Beginning: Playing and Working with Words

Young children engage in wordplay from the moment they start to babble. They play with sounds, they mimic intonation, they listen to the rhythm of language, and they begin to speak.

Rhyming comes as naturally to them as breathing, and they rhyme real words with nonsense words. They might say, *la, la, la, ga, ga, ga*, but when they come to *ma, ma, ma*, they get such an amazing reaction that they repeat the pattern again and again, much to their mother's delight. The same applies to *da, da, da*. Then both parents are equally happy!

The task for the teacher is to harness this love of words and the sounds of language into daily opportunities for wordplay. Why? Because wordplay is a base for word work in spelling.

Rhyme and Pattern

Rhyme is often the place to begin as children either know many rhymes and jingles already or will most definitely be exposed to them in school. Skipping rhymes and jingles have been passed down through an oral tradition for generations. Children learn them in the schoolyard as well as in the classroom. So, they just need to learn that certain words rhyme and be able to give examples with ease.

They can fill in blanks for various kinds of rhymes:

- For a counting rhyme:

  One potato, two potato,
  Three potato, *four,*
  Five potato, six potato,
  Seven potato, _____. [*more*]

- For a skipping rhyme:

  Apples, peaches, pears, and plums,
  Tell me when my birthday comes.
  [The rope is then turned quickly, while saying the months of the year, with the skipper ending on her birthday.]

- For a traditional rhyme:

  Humpty Dumpty sat on a wall,
  Humpty Dumpty had a great _____. [*fall*]

International Rhymes

For a list of international rhymes, check out www.mamalisa.com, which you can view in English, French, or Spanish.

Beyond traditional rhymes, we need to expand our repertoire to better match the lives and experiences of our students. With children arriving almost daily from every part of the world, it is important to share or, if necessary, create rhymes about common experiences.

You can demonstrate that many traditional rhymes are about everyday experiences. For example:

> Rain, rain, go away,
> Come again another _____. [*day*]

Then, with the children, you can co-construct rhymes along these lines:

> I like to run, and jump, and play.
> Yes, I love recess every day!

> I caught a frog.
> I called him Tad.
> I brought him home.
> My mom got _____. [mad; *or* My dad was _____.]

Teachers of young children play with rhymes many times during the day. It would add variety if you sometimes turn a rhyme into a *cloze* activity, where students fill in the blanks, as above. You can thereby link student thought to rhyme and help students generate rhyming words.

Wordplay and Technology

Wordplay and technology combine well on the following sites.

Wordle: This is the best-known cloud generator for wordplay. It is free and has editing capabilities. You do not need to log in or provide your email address.
http://www.wordle.net/create

Word It Out: This free site is similar to Wordle, except you can ignore certain words and keep them out. You can customize the word cloud by font, size, and color. The saving option requires email.
http://worditout.com/

Tag Crowd: This free and easy-to-use site shows frequency of words in alphabetical order. It lacks the color and layout variation of Wordle, but because of this, it might be easier to use with younger students. No login or email address is required.
http://tagcrowd.com/

The Alphabet Letter–Sound Link

Another link that young children have to make in Kindergarten and Grade 1 is that between letters of the alphabet and their sounds.

First of all, they need to learn the names of the alphabet letters, and the easiest place to start is with the first letter of their first name. Since everything is labeled from their coat hooks to their running shoes, most children can locate that letter and trace it with a finger. Naming the letters is different from learning the sounds of letters, though. Depending on their motivation, some children may learn some sounds first.

Bear in mind that children have diverse learning styles. Some struggle to learn any sound in isolation, so it may be a good idea to deal with letters at the beginning of words and the sounds they make. Again, students' names, both first and last, are a great source of study. Students come to notice, for example, that *James* and *John* begin with the same letter, but *Sam* does not; *Nimrit* and *Noor* begin with the same letter, but *Jatinder* does not, and so on.

Many teachers of young children create authentic reasons for their students to write to people. For example, the teacher and a group of students might come together to co-create a thank-you letter to Tim Hortons after they had a field trip there. Or, a similar letter could be constructed after a trip to a large store, with perhaps a short report or classroom map attached to show how the students turned the classroom into a large store with a variety of merchandise. Typically, the teacher leads the students to review meaning first and then, if writing a letter, perhaps reviews simple form. Word work in small groups would come later.

Young children often come together for a read-aloud experience. The teacher may select a book that can be shared and read a poem or narrative from it to the children. She could then make a small group or have children self-select to join to do some Shared Reading, using a small part of the book's text. For word work, children could be asked to think of a word that begins with the same letter as a word in this small part of the text. Alternatively, they could generate words that rhyme with a word from the text that either they or the teacher has chosen. If this activity is presented in the form of a game, children will be almost unaware of how much they are learning. This kind of exploration lays an important foundation for word structure and word sense. Teachers of young children are often masterful at games involving wordplay.

Students in the last part of Kindergarten or early Grade 1 should be comfortable with rhyme and either able to supply rhyming words, as introduced above, or create the second line to a chant.

> Share toys every day.
> *Yes, when we go out to play.*

By this time, I find, students usually know many letter names and a fair number of sounds. They may be able to suggest the beginning sound of a word when their teacher writes on a chart, whiteboard, or paper under the document camera. If the students don't know any of this, the teacher can engage in differentiated instruction, beginning where they are and taking them forward from there.

Beginning letters and sounds

For children who already know many beginning sounds, the teacher can review or teach consonants, sometimes beginning with *m, n, f,* or *s,* as these sounds can be pronounced in isolation with the least distortion; however, be sure to teach letters in an order that works: one related to student interest and motivation. It is also important to separate letters that are visually confusing, such as *b* and *d,* and *p* and *g* (*q* is usually taught with *u,* so it does not get confused with *p*). At this time, it is comforting for students to know that the letter names never change, although the sounds of the letters (as in *cent* and *cage*) do.

Students can also create simpler two-word phrases such as "big bears," "pretty butterflies," and "noisy bees."

- Alphabet books are useful here, for letter recognition and instruction, especially if they have more than one word or illustration for each letter. Students can add their names and suggest words that match the beginning sound of the page you are highlighting. The play aspect of language needs to be emphasized here.
- Real objects are also helpful for wordplay. You can have a bag or mystery box with several objects whose names begin with the consonant being taught. As you pull out the object, students guess the word and isolate the first letter. Students can co-create two-word sentences with you, using the words from the objects. For example: Bears bump. Butterflies balance. Bees buzz.

  Students need to build vocabulary, too. They can extend their two-word sentences, coming up with variations like these or versions that will range from the simple to the more complex: Bears bump clumsily, butterflies balance perfectly, and bees buzz busily. Wordplay is work at multiple levels.
- Linking tongue twisters to beginning sounds can be fun, as long as the tongue twisters are not too difficult — "She sells sea shells" is a standard. If children live miles inland and have never seen the sea, though, they might find it more meaningful to co-construct tongue twisters with the teacher. Here are three good samples of tongue-twister wordplay:

Two Sources of Tongue Twisters
www.indianchild.com/tongue_twisters.htm
http://learnenglishkids.british council.org/en/tongue-twisters

big black backpacks on the blue coat rack
short shoelaces on six shoes
picking up popcorn perfectly

Children begin to lose front teeth around this time, and as a result, can begin to think that the word *rabbit* begins with *w*, for example, because that is what they hear when they try to sound it out. They do not always enunciate clearly, either. Having a foam letter or a magnetic letter for them to manipulate, as well as encouraging them to speak clearly, can be helpful.

Building a word wall

As students become comfortable with beginning sounds, you can prompt them to listen for the same sound at the end of words. While learning to identify the ending sounds, they can begin to help construct simple words for the class word wall. Many primary classrooms (Grades 1 to 3) have word walls, and some classrooms with older students have them, as well.

A *word wall* is an organized collection of words displayed at eye level in the classroom. The words are usually placed in alphabetical order, and their purpose is to teach students to read and spell the most common words, and to see patterns and relationships among words. A word wall is built by students with the help of the teacher.

The words on a word wall are used as an interactive tool. If young children add the word *can* to the word wall, they can identify the letters *c* and *n* and the teacher can supply the vowel. Or, the students can guess what the vowel might be as there are only five (and sometimes *y*) to choose from. (It is even possible to introduce short vowels at this stage so that students can combine consonants and vowels to create simple words.) Students can identify words that rhyme with *can* and create couplets: think of "The Little Engine That Could."

I think I can!
I think I can! . . .

or

"Bring me a fan."
"Of course, I can!"

The website www.dltk-kids.com/ type/word-wall-words.htm offers ready-made templates that you may find useful when developing a word wall.

For the word wall to be successful, it must be more than an alphabetical list of words on cards on a wall. If that's all it is, it will be ignored by students — they will see it as wallpaper. Ideally, students should be able to take the words down from the wall (Velcro helps here as do magnets if using a magnetic whiteboard). Students can then copy the words and create other words that start or end as they do, have the same vowels as they do, have the same number of letters as they do, or rhyme with one of them. When students are older, they may choose a word from the word wall and create other words with double consonants or contractions, or that are compound in structure. There are all sorts of possibilities.

In *What Really Matters in Spelling?* author Patricia Cunningham links common words to a word wall and emphasizes the importance of patterns in the words. Spelling them is not enough; students need to apply their spelling knowledge to words of the same pattern.

An excellent idea is for the teacher to access a list of 50 common words in student writing and to add them slowly to the word wall, working with them as they are added. For example, if you were adding the word *big* to the word wall, you would ask students if they know the beginning letter and the ending letter, and invite them to guess the vowel. Then, you would prompt them to suggest rhyming words for *big*. Later, if a student wanted to write the word *pig*, he could be reminded that it rhymes with *big* but has a different beginning letter. Then the student could take the word *big* from the word wall and make an informed guess on how to spell the word *pig* correctly. This practice not only boosts student confidence but gives an anchor word and a strategy for writing *wig* or *dig*. The student is coming to know a simple rhyming pattern that fits a series of words.

The term *anchor word* refers to a word on the word wall that is linked to rhyme and word construction. For example, *big* could be the anchor word for *wig, dig, fig*, and *jig*.

As students learn to create rhyming words from an anchor word by changing only the first letter, they notice that they can apply this pattern to quite a few words. They develop a sense of generalization. For young children, gaining this sense is empowering, and for young writers, it is encouraging because it puts them in charge of the learning. Students with this awareness have entered an early stage of what is called "spelling consciousness."

The Basics of Phonological Knowledge

As students build consciousness of how words work, they need to develop *phonological knowledge*, or the ability to hear, recognize, and combine different sounds, over time and with practice. To do this they need

You are more likely to be familiar with the idea of word families than with the terms *onset* and *rime*. You may want to look up lists of common onsets and rimes on the Internet. For example, here is one good source: www.wilkinsfarago.com.au/PDFs/ Reading_Spelling_Lists.pdf.

- the ability to identify words as single units, as opposed to strings of letters
- the ability to identify syllables in the rhythm of language, which they can do by clapping to chants and songs, and by reproducing rhythms clapped by the teacher (e.g., sun-ny — 2 claps; sun — 1 clap)
- the ability to recognize specific letters and sounds and know where they occur in a word (e.g., in the word *flame*, "fl" is the blend or onset at the beginning of a word, and "ame" is the rime at the end, the part of the word that follows the onset and includes the vowel)

Phonemic Knowledge

Phonemic knowledge is auditory only. It involves the ability to blend and segment sounds. Students need to be able to hear sounds at the beginnings and endings of words. For example, they would need to blend the sounds /mmm aaa dd/ into *mad* and to segment by hearing, then identifying, /m/ at the beginning and /d/ at the end of the word *mad*. Students may enjoy standing apart, holding the individual letters *m, a,* and *d,* and then coming together to say the word — movement often helps memory. Bear in mind that children are not limited to using simple words like this — the words are short and simple only to help them hear the sounds.

One of the better known lists of rimes was developed by Wylie and Durrell in 1970. See page 27 in Chapter 2.

A consonant digraph consists of two letters that represent one sound, for example, *ch, sh, th,* and *wh.* There are also vowel digraphs, for example, *ea* in *meat.*

- the ability to hear and manipulate sounds by blending and segmenting them, based on knowing that words are composed of individual sounds, or phonemes (phonemic knowledge)

The following chart is intended to help clarify the linguistic ideas above. It reads across, highlighting the development of a particular skill. Its purpose is to enable teachers to help students acquire more phonological knowledge. It could be used or modified to help with planning next steps or determining where students are on an informal spelling continuum, which moves from less difficult to more difficult.

Phonological Knowledge

less difficult ———————————————————————→ *more difficult*

POSITION OF LETTER IN A WORD	Initial Consonant	Final Consonant	Medial Consonant
Simple rhyming words	can identify and match rhyming words Teacher might ask, "Do these two words rhyme? *pat, sat*" "Do these two words rhyme? *fill, fog*" (Student can show thumbs up for correct, thumbs down for incorrect.)	can identify which word does not belong in a set of rhyming words Teacher might ask, "Which word does not rhyme with *mad*? *sad, sat, glad*" "Which word does not belong? *rough, tough, love, enough*"	can independently suggest words that rhyme Student can independently state, "*Mist* rhymes with *fist, list,* and *wrist.*"
Syllable knowledge	can clap out syllables in words with rhythm, modelled by teacher (e.g., "Ted-dy bear" clapped three times)	can clap two sounds for two-syllable words, when the teacher says the word (e.g., "sun-ny")	can identify the sounds of syllables in three-syllable words independently, as in "won-der-ful"
Moving from simple to more complex rhymes	using anchor words to start rhyming word lists; sample anchor words are *run, can, jump, make, top,* and *fill.* The teacher could add many simple words from rhymes and chants.	exploring rhyming words with blends (e.g., *spell, drink, slice*), digraphs (e.g., *thank, blank, drank*), and word pairs with different vowel spellings for the same sound (e.g., *ball, loss; sky, lie*).	exploring more complex rhymes (e.g., *boy, coil; each, sheet; sunny, wonder; shock, walk*) Alternative pairs that are either visually similar or with the same sound but different spelling are explored.

Foundations of Awareness

Having a plan with broad parameters is necessary to give students a strong foundation and to help build their spelling consciousness. It would be appropriate to adopt an approach where students are introduced to concepts, sometimes because they are interested in certain patterns and other times because the teacher feels that, based on oral or written samples, there is a definite need. The teacher would later circle back to consolidate this learning.

As well as having phonological knowledge, students need three other kinds of knowledge about words in a spelling context: graphophonic (which relates to the sound of words and how they look), syntactic (which relates to syntax, for example, *-ed* verb endings), and semantic (which relates to meaning, including word origins).

Graphophonic knowledge is the ability to learn sound–symbol relationships. Students need to realize that the letter name always stays the same, but sounds can change and letters can combine to make new sounds. This is the alphabetic principle of language, where multiple letters are combined to make the same sound. English has 26 letters and more than 40 sounds.

Syntactic knowledge is the ability to build knowledge of the structure and function of words, and to understand words in their smallest parts. To increase knowledge, students need to explore the formation of plurals, comparatives, inflectional endings, compound words, and contractions.

Semantic knowledge pertains to the meanings or definitions of words, and their origins. This kind of knowledge helps students to understand where words have come from and provides them with more idea of how to make sense of English spelling. It relates to prefixes and suffixes, and how these connect to base words.

less difficult ——————————————————→ more difficult		
Graphophonic Knowledge	**Syntactic Knowledge**	**Semantic Knowledge**
sound and visual appearance of words	grammatical function and syntax of words	meaning, derivation, and origin of words

Spelling is developmental, and the students in any one class are in different developmental phases. Many students come to school with a great deal of knowledge of words and how they work. Other students know little about how words work. This is where teachers can close the gap: by building word knowledge for everyone.

An Evolving Spelling Consciousness

We want to give students many opportunities to write so that they can experiment with how to spell different words and learn how words work. Consider what this writing sample from the end of Senior Kindergarten can tell us.

Sidebar:

Many children will have developed strong graphophonic knowledge by the end of Grade 2 or earlier. They can try to write most words, and as they learn more about language, their accuracy in spelling will increase.

This student knows the beginning, ending, and medial sounds of this word, *soccer*. He chose *k* to represent the sound /k/, and it does represent the sound correctly. Some children would still be writing random letters, and a few may even write more than this. At this stage, the goal is to celebrate where students are and to encourage them to keep writing.

As students learn more about words, they move along the learning continuum, but their progress is not always recognized. Often, as students write longer pieces with more approximate spelling, their parents say that they are misspelling more words. To address such concerns, it is useful to dictate a short piece of text that the child wrote earlier in the year, so that you can demonstrate improvement.

One six-year-old wrote this in September in Grade 1:

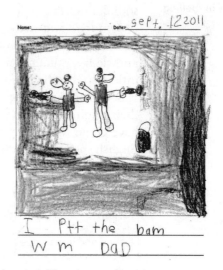

I Ptt the bam w m DaD [I paint the bathroom with my dad.]

When this sentence was dictated in June at the end of Grade 1, the student wrote:

I pint the bathroom whit my dad.

When I asked the child what he had learned, he said, "I know how to spell 'paint' now, and 'bathroom.'" He did know how to spell *bathroom*, and he was missing only one vowel in *paint*, but he had transposed some letters in *with*, indicating that he had not yet internalized that word. Nonetheless, he had moved along on his journey to more accurate spelling. Through the dictation of the earlier piece, both parents and student could recognize the progress.

Because this same Grade 1 student had been given many opportunities to write and was able to construct words from an increasing knowledge of how words work, he was able to write this piece about six weeks into second term. The initial prompt was given by the teacher, and by this time, he had been taught how to sequence and write a conclusion. Here is the text of his writing, which was spread over three pages with a picture on the top of the first page.

> There are three interesting winter activities I like to do. First I like to go boggon. win I go toboggan I hiv to not fol dan. and I hiv to not go on the big bop. Second I like to mik sow ihol. Win I mik my sow ihol I hriy to not sap on my sow ihol. I mik six sow ihol. Lastly I like to hovul the snw. Win I hovel the snow I like to pic los a snow. These are the three interesting winter activities I like to do.

The student knows these common words: *I, like, to go, not, on, my, the, to, do, first, second,* and *lastly.* After a number of approximations, he spelled *snow* correctly, and he was very close to *toboggan.* He also had "hovel" for *shovel.* Mostly, he is linking letters to sound. "hriy" is interesting for *try.* Young children also write "chran" for *train,* because they find the /r/ sound difficult.

Here is a standard English translation of the above piece of writing:

> There are three interesting winter activities I like to do. First I like to toboggan. When I go tobogganing I have to not fall down. And I have to not go on the big bump. Second I like to make snow angels. When I make my snow angel I try to not step on my snow angel. I make six snow angel. Lastly I like to shovel the snow. When I shovel the snow I like to pack lots of snow. These are the three interesting winter activities I like to do.

This work has been done independently, with the first and last sentences supplied by the teacher. This student has experienced much growth since writing "I Ptt the bam w m DaD" four months earlier.

Another student in the same Grade 1 class wrote this in September:

> On the weekend I was sike.

Apart from the word *sick*, every word is spelled correctly, and it is interesting to note where this student was at the end of Grade 1, when he created an Energy booklet, with headings provided by the teacher. This student has exceptional spelling consciousness.

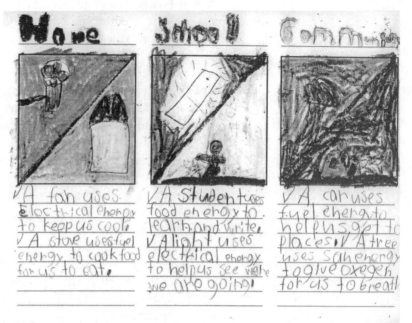

Home	School	Community
A fan uses electrical energy to keep us cool. A stove uses fuel energy to cook food for us to eat.	A student uses food energy to learn and write. A light uses electrical energy to help us see **were** we are going.	A car uses fuel energy to help us get to places. A tree uses sun energy to give **oxegen** for us to **breath**.

Because of many opportunities to write a variety of texts, this student has become an engaged writer who has learned a great deal about how words work. His Energy booklet shows how he is now integrating his spelling knowledge into Science, a cross-curricular piece of writing.

Another student, given the same task, wrote this (translations next page):

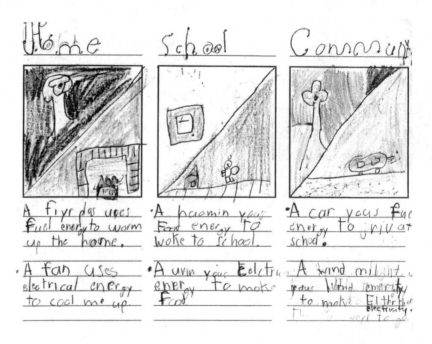

Home	School	Community
A fireplace uses fuel energy to warm up the house. A fan uses electrical energy to cool me up.	A human uses food energy to walk to school. An oven uses electrical energy to make food.	A car uses fuel energy to drive at school. A windmill uses wind energy to make electricity.

This student may be more typical of Grade 1 students you know. He does not always use the word wall because *electrical* is spelled correctly just once, and *energy* is spelled correctly multiple times. You can see the attempt to match sounds to written words in "fiyr plas" for *fireplace*, "haomin" for *human*, "uvin" for *oven*, and "jriv" for *drive*. This student has also come a long way from writing " I P B" (I played Beyblades) at the beginning of the year.

In Grade 1, we are helping students develop writing fluency with multiple text forms and multiple purposes for writing, but as students go through the grades, there are basic skills we want them to acquire. Where do we go from here?

I played Beyblades.

What to Look For on a Developmental Journey

By the end of Grade 6, you would expect students to be familiar with sound, function, and meaning patterns, to have acquired word knowledge over time and in context, and to be able to apply this knowledge directly to editing their written work. A great deal of practice will be involved. As students investigate word patterns, asking questions about words and noticing how words work, they will come close to conventional spelling and will make more refined predictions about how to spell new words. Their spelling consciousness will increase to the point where they can identify a number of misspelled words and suggest corrections from their knowledge of how words are constructed.

The scales below show the movement across students' acquisition of word knowledge, from less difficult to more difficult, which they need to know or be familiar with by the end of Grade 6.

Five Developmental Scales

less difficult ⟶ *more difficult*

knowledge of frequently used words   knowledge of less common words

less difficult ⟶ *more difficult*

single vowels (e.g., b**a**t)   vowel pairs (e.g., p**ea**ch)

less difficult ⟶ *more difficult*

rhyming relationships (e.g., b**and**, s**and**)   derivational relationships (e.g., si**gn**, si**gn**ature)

less difficult ⟶ *more difficult*

recognition of word patterns   recognition of word origins

less difficult ⟶ *more difficult*

playing with words (word games)   making plays on words (e.g., puns)

2

Teaching Spelling Through Writing: Finding the Balance

In Chapter 1, I have shown the initial stages of spelling consciousness through working with words, but it cannot be overemphasized that the purpose to use accurate spelling to communicate clearly is found in writing. As soon as children begin to write, they become more aware of the importance of clear communication. As they work through the developmental stages of spelling to standard spelling, they learn more and more about how words can be constructed.

The Building Blocks for Spelling Success

The chart below provides an outline of how children's knowledge of spelling develops.

Spelling Development: Building Graphophonic Knowledge VS (Visual + Sound)						
less difficult ─── →*more difficult*						
scribbling to represent a message	making random letters to convey meaning	matching sounds and letters to produce (1) initial consonants; (2) final consonants; (3) medial consonants; combining onsets and common rimes (e.g., initial consonants with *-at, -ump, -an, -ill, -in, -it*) demonstrating attempts to include short vowels	consolidating knowledge of short vowels and adding *y* as sometimes being a vowel; combining onsets (e.g., consonant-blended letters *bl, br, cl, cr, dr, gl, gr, pl, pr, str, spr*) and consonant digraphs *ch, sh, th, wh,* and *ph* with simple rimes	knowing all short vowels, plus *y*; learning about possibilities for long vowels; combining onsets with rimes, also called "word families" (e.g., *back, lack, black, slack, crack*)	demonstrating knowledge of long vowels and some vowel pairs; exploring more complex onsets and rimes; beginning to predict how words might be spelled with some accuracy	showing their knowledge about choices of vowel pairs (e.g., *oi* or *oy*) to match a sound; adding to their growing word knowledge; demonstrating that their predictions on how words are spelled are more accurate

Building Graphophonic Knowledge: Students in Grade 1 and early Grade 2 are able to approximate the spellings of many words as they build knowledge of onsets (consonants, consonant clusters, and consonant digraphs) and as they become familiar with short vowels. They use visual information combined with sound (referred to as **V S**) to do this. They are thereby set up for success in spelling, as students who spell well mentally record visual information, which they can recall later. Students who have poor visual memories tend to find spelling extremely difficult until they discover it does not rely on rote memory, but on thinking about patterns and learning about how words work. This building of sound and visual knowledge needs to be done, however, in the context of learning to write to communicate.

Common Onsets

As noted earlier, the term *onset* refers to the beginning of a word before the vowel. Common onsets include the following:
- all single consonants
- initial consonant blends: bl, cl, fl, gl, pl, sl; br, cr, dr, fr, gr, pr, tr, wr; sc, sk, sm, sn, sp, st; sw, tw; spl, scr, spr, str

Common onsets also include these:
- consonant digraphs (a pair of letters representing one sound): ch, sh, th, wh, ph
- consonant combinations: shr, thr, sch, squ

Without purposeful communication, there is no real need for spelling, and without building word knowledge, there is no way of understanding how words work. Therefore, spelling needs to be viewed both by teacher and student as a tool of the writing process, with its own place and importance.

Helping Students Make the Bridge Between Spelling and Writing

As students write, they need to focus on composing and revising their writing at separate times. They also need to attend to form — writing a report or an explanation is very different from writing a narrative. As they begin their writing, they need to have a basic knowledge of how to form words, and this knowledge should grow daily. However, if teachers overfocus on accuracy at the composing stage, it can inhibit the ability of the student to formulate ideas and generate language. When the content is complete, *then* spelling needs to be a major focus, as the writer proofreads, questions certain spellings, then checks and self-corrects, or consults a peer, the dictionary, or the teacher.

Fledgling writers need to use prior knowledge of words, choose a spelling pattern from available options, and then test this spelling hypothesis in an effort to convey meaning in print. For example, if students know that -*ly* is a suffix that is added to a word, then they will not worry about doubling letters in that particular case — they simply take the word *total* and add -*ly* to be totally correct.

When a student learns to spell a word in context, research shows that the word is not only more likely to be retained, but that it is more likely to be used correctly in written work.

The problem is that many students are unable to identify words that they have misspelled. Editing becomes so onerous that they get discouraged or lose confidence. Editing involves checking and correcting spelling, punctuation, and grammar, and that further complicates the issue. Nonetheless, it is possible to help children edit for spelling by having them look *for only one thing at a time*. By doing so, they will experience success and grow to become better spellers and more accurate editors. Within the writing program, teachers gain more practice reading and editing work than students do, but students are the ones who need to practise. Students require a number of strategies, as they cannot edit for more than one or two items at a time until later in their schooling.

How to Edit for Commonly Misspelled Words

Many years ago Ves Thomas completed a study among Canadian children and found the 100 most commonly misspelled words in writing. I will give examples of words misspelled in Grades 1 through 3, and Grades 4 through 6 so that you can clearly see the overlap. The words are listed in descending order of frequent misspellings.

To help students edit more successfully, you could provide a list of five of these words and have students look for them in their writing to check if they were misspelled. Compared to looking for every word misspelled, this task is simple for a student. I have found that students in Grade 1 are working hard just to produce writing. Although they can produce more than one draft, they are not interested in editing, and developmentally, editing is not appropriate for them. Instead, the teacher can conference with them and build word knowledge while demonstrating simple editing. So, the time to begin this activity is in mid to late Grade 2 at the earliest, depending on the maturity of the students. Since students at the end of Grade 2 are still producing fairly short pieces of writing, it would not take them too long to look for five words, one word at a time.

If you feel that a word such as *straw*, which appears on the Grade 1 list, no longer applies to your students, look for a more current list.

Grade 1	Grade 2	Grade 3
too	too	too
they	because	because
to	upon	friend
friend	they	that's
goes	wheels	through
because	about	there
little	again	upon
said	didn't	went
straw	holiday	where
teacher	said	finally
was	scared	wait
nice	that's	am
like	to	first
there	ghost	it's

Grade 1	Grade 2	Grade 3
have	good-bye	another
when	morning	clothes
wants	our	know
I	people	said
eat	dead	their
sometimes	many	were

Source: From THOMAS. Teaching Spelling — Second Edition, 2E. © 1979 Nelson Education Ltd. Reproduced by permission. www.cengage.com/permissions.

If students are still writing "woz" or "wos" for *was*, or "bekos" for *because*, they are focusing entirely on sound and not on visual appearance. A mini-lesson here would remind students that paying attention to how the word looks is important too. This idea applies to any misspelled words where students are relying on sound. They need to learn to use a visual exercise, so it would be good to provide them with a strategy, like the one below, or some modification of it. Combinations of this strategy, the shortest being "Look-Write-Cover-Check," have been used for years, but these four words do not convey the whole story, and we have learned that multiple strategies are important as they work well for different children.

> Look at the word.
> Say the word aloud, spelling out each letter.
> Picture the word in your mind.
> Cover the word.
> Picture the word again. (Students can also subvocalize the letters, or trace the letters on one hand.)
> Write the word.
> Check that the word is spelled correctly.

Instead of visualizing the word a second time, students could be encouraged to subvocalize or trace the letters. Either of these approaches allows students who have alternative learning styles to link to their memories. This exercise would be done only for a few words at a time.

Students in Grades 4, 5, and 6 could have a list of more than five words but no more than 10 words, still looking for one or two of them at a time. Lists such as those below are not spelling lists, but editing checklists for commonly misspelled words.

Grade 4	Grade 5	Grade 6
their	too	their
through	that's	too
because	until	that's

Grade 4	Grade 5	Grade 6
friend	there	friend
too	lot	it's
an	you're	lot
off	silver	there
that's	beautiful	our
they	it's	beautiful
there	friend	grabbed
heard	chief	heard
know	again	outside
finally	holiday	then
again	horror	they
course	off	you're
then	quite	finally
went	received	pollution
caught	they	started
told	stubborn	people
think	started	supper

Source: From THOMAS. Teaching Spelling — Second Edition, 2E. © 1979 Nelson Education Ltd. Reproduced by permission. www.cengage.com/permissions.

The link to writing is essential, as spelling in isolation does not ensure application. The Ves Thomas list is one of the few Canadian sources, but you can find many lists of commonly misspelled words online to use for this editing activity. It will encourage you to know that lists of misspellings such as the Ves Thomas one were collected when students were involved in a formal spelling program. Students were exposed to approximately 3000 words from Grades 2 to 6, to be learned by rote. Note that after this formal instruction, the word *too* dropped from first place in Grade 2 to second place in Grade 6; in Grade 6, *their* topped the list of misspelled words. As I noted previously, that word is more likely to have been misused than misspelled, but the result is still an error. This history suggests that it would be fairly low risk for you to try to raise students' spelling consciousness by the ways I suggest in this book, rather than to engage students in rote memorization, which often does not transfer to written work.

Please make sure that you do not choose words from a list of words that children have trouble reading, as that is a different list and would not apply directly to writing.

Sample Online Sources of Commonly Misspelled Words

http://academic.cuesta.edu/
acasupp/as/819.htm
www.teachingideas.co.uk/english/
misspelled.htm

Creating a school word list of commonly misspelled words

One way of personalizing a list of commonly misspelled words is to keep track of which words you find in student writing that are commonly misspelled across Grades 4, 5, and 6 in your school. From Grade 4 onward, teachers at each grade level could look for commonly misspelled words in student writing and list them. Teachers would then compare lists across Grade 4 and reach consensus on common misspellings. This work would be repeated in Grades 5 and 6. The teachers in the junior division (Grades 4 through 6) would then get together to share their 50 to 60 most commonly misspelled words, to be used for editing by the students. The list could be adjusted from year to year, depending on whether or not teachers found the same misspelled words occurring.

You could involve students in the task of identifying the words, too. There could be a class discussion on commonly misspelled words. Students I have talked to in Grade 4 and up identify words such as *their* and *there*, which they more often misuse than misspell, but, of course, if used in the wrong context, the word is misspelled. They say that listing *there* with *where, somewhere*, and *anywhere* sometimes helps them to remember which one to use. They also recognize *friend* as a word they have a problem with because they omit the *i* or are unsure of its placement; furthermore, they identify that they are unsure where to put the apostrophe in words such as *it's, don't*, and *didn't*, indicating that they are having problems with contractions. Several mini-lessons on contractions would help resolve this problem. This type of discussion with the teacher about words brings cognition and word awareness to the context of spelling, and, I found, students become better at self-identifying and self-correcting misspelled words if they are actively aware of words that they frequently misspell.

It would be worthwhile, as well, to see how your school's lists compare to lists by Ves Thomas and others, and whether there is much variance from year to year. There would be variance in word usage, as children write about a variety of topics, and there are always words that specifically interest them. However, your school would have developed a custom list of misspelled words, taken from the children's writing. As students master how to spell these words, the school newsletter could provide an excellent statistic, for example: "Seventy percent of students in Grades 4, 5, and 6 have mastered commonly misspelled words at their grade level. This percentage is growing daily. Please look at our bulletin boards when you visit the school for samples of student writing."

Being able to spell well is a combination of acquiring word knowledge over time and applying it directly to writing. The goal is to have students who are able to make more refined predictions about the spelling of a word from a growing knowledge of patterns in words.

Approaching Spelling Patterns Through Investigation and Inquiry

Later in this book, function and meaning patterns will be addressed, as well.

Patterns occur in nature and in numbers; thus, it appeals to logical thinking that there are both sound and meaning patterns in words. Children can engage in inquiry through many activities related to sound patterns. Generating questions is one activity, and these questions or investigations can be modeled by the teacher, co-created by the teacher and student, or generated by the students. Students gravitate to making meaning.

Applying an inquiry mindset to spelling creates a way for students to feel in control of their learning. They can too easily feel that there are so many exceptions to spelling patterns that they are adrift in a sea of words. To be problem solvers with words is much more interesting than to try repeatedly to memorize words out of context — a problem-solving approach also has more carry-over to successful application.

Plan to create inquiry activities or investigations related to sound patterns. If students have never done this before, the first patterns should be relatively straightforward and initially generated by you interacting with students and giving them clues. Later, students could devise questions to investigate. It is recommended that they work in pairs and perhaps come back to this activity over a period of days. Note that the key difference between an investigation and an inquiry is that an investigation is more teacher generated and possibly less openended, while an inquiry could be teacher or student generated, and is definitely more open-ended.

Here are a few sample investigations, expressed from a student's point of view.

> **Investigation 1:** Take two consonants — *b*, *c* — and make sets of rhyming endings for them (e.g., *bat*, *cat*; *ban*, *can*). What strategy did you use to find words?

Investigation 1 examples: *bore, core; bone, cone; bake, cake; bash, cash*

> **Investigation 2:** Take two consonants — *g*, *l* — and make sets of rhyming endings for them (e.g., *game, lame*). Did you use the dictionary? Did you have another strategy? What was it?

Investigation 2 examples: *gate, late; gore, lore; got, lot; gap, lap; guck, luck; gash, lash*

Multiple consonants can be listed in twos or threes to create investigations like the two above. An alternative to this investigation is to take a rhyming pair, for example, *game* and *lame*, and see whether students could create a list using many beginning consonants (*came, dame, fame, name, same, tame*). This activity is easier and might help as a parallel task to differentiate while working on rhyming words.

> **Investigation 3:** Take two consonant pairs — *st* and *tr* — and make sets of rhyming endings for them (e.g., *stain, train*; *stay, tray*). Did you need to look at a list of vowel pairs to help you? Did you have another strategy?

Investigation 3 is easier than Investigation 4 because students have only two blends to consider as they explore endings (*stack, track; stump, trump; stay, tray; stick, trick; stuck, truck; stash, trash*). Let students know that using a dictionary is helpful, not cheating. However, tell students that you would like them to try to generate the words on their own before turning to a dictionary. Multiple similar investigations or inquiry questions could be generated, using two consonant pairs.

Beyond prompting students to use rhymes to solve inquiry questions, be sure to have them use rhymes in wordplay and riddles. Students will remember the wordplay aspect of language long after they have built word families.

> **Investigation 4:** Take three consonant pairs—*bl*, *sn*, and *st*—and try to make sets of rhyming endings for at least two of them (e.g., *black, snack, stack*). Explain which consonant pair you found easiest to create your lists.

Investigation 4 examples: *blink, stink; snore, store; block, stock; bling, sting*

Investigation 4 is definitely a thinking activity as well as one involving sound; it can be made easier or harder, depending on the sets of consonants used.

Encourage students to have multiple strategies for generating words. Referring to a list would be one alternative to the dictionary strategy. Students will enjoy the challenge of finding other strategies, such as checking the word wall, checking word lists on display in the classroom, checking personal word lists, and creating lists of rimes.

Below is a list of common endings.

37 COMMON RIMES

ack	ail	ain
ake	ale	ame
an	ank	ap
ash	at	ate
aw	ay	eat
ell	est	ice
ick	ide	ight
ill	in	ine
in	ink	ip
it	ock	oke
op	ore	ot
uck	ug	ump
unk		

Source: Wylie, R. E., and D. D. Durrell. 1970. "Teaching Vowels Through Phonograms." *Elementary English* 47: 787–91; cited in *Literacy Strategies for Grades 4–12: Reinforcing the Threads of Reading* by Karen Tankersley (Alexandria, VA: Association for Supervision and Curriculum Development, 2005).

Wylie and Durrell (1970) list 37 of the most common rimes (formerly called "word families"). They have said that their list can be used to generate 500 English words. The Internet provides many lists of common rimes, but most of these are based on Wylie and Durrell's original list.

A variety of inquiries

All students learn differently, so when students are given the task to generate words, it is often good to have parallel tasks with a focus on the same topic.

Rimes and Rhyming Words

A rime is the end of a word including the vowel, and it can be used to create word families. For example, from the rime *-all* you can create *ball, call, fall, hall, mall, tall,* and *wall*. Rhyming words can have different spellings. They rely totally on sound, as in *there, fare,* and *pair*. Rhyming words can be spelled the same way or not; rimes are always spelled the same way.

Students will likely recognize this strategy of providing parallel tasks because it is used in Mathematics. To give choice, there may be questions labeled A and B, with no reference to less difficult and more difficult. This neutral approach is important as we would not want to stigmatize a student who chooses the easier question.

> **Inquiry A1:** Here are two digraphs — *ch* and *sh*. List some words that begin with these digraphs and some words that end with them. You may work with a partner.

Inquiry A1 is more straightforward than Inquiry A2, below. You could either use your professional judgment about which students do which inquiry, or allow them to choose. They are working on similar goals.

> **Inquiry A2:** For the digraphs *ch*, *sh*, *th*, and *wh*, list words that begin with each and end with each. In addition, can you identify at least one word that begins and ends with the same digraph? You may work with a partner to generate these words.

Here are just a few examples for each of the three categories (beginning, end, and both), noted above. If given time, students will come up with many more.

chew	shoe	think	what
chop	shirt	than	where
chug	short	thug	when
chill	shot	thin	why
choke	shock	thump	wheat
much	mush	teeth	*no words found*
such	dish	wreath	
church	shush	thirteenth	*no words found*

Here, we move to more open-ended work with inquiry.

> **Inquiry B1:** Predict whether there are more words containing *ai* or *ay*. Generate lists and keep adding to them. What were your findings? Did any words surprise you?

At least 3500 words contain *ai*, and more than 1200 words contain *ay*, which more usually appears at the end of a word, for example, *play, say, ray, stay, hay,* and *display*. Student findings may vary. After a number of them have shared their findings, encourage them to try to figure out which of the two-vowel combinations appears in most words. They could begin with a class survey; if carried across the grade level, the data could be quite interesting.

> **Inquiry B2:** Predict whether more words end in *-eat* or *-ate*. Create a table and add to it. One word merges them both together. Can you find it?

Create a Riddle
A Grade 5 student asked me which word merges -*eat* and -*ate*. Luckily, I was able to solve the riddle quickly, for which I am grateful! The word that merges both -*eat* and -*ate* is *create*. Encourage your students to generate riddles related to words.

Far more words end with -*ate* and students, I find, seem to endlessly enjoy adding to this list. This type of work could be linked to gathering data from other students, as in the inquiry outlined below.

> **Inquiry C:** With a partner, survey each student in your class, asking which two words they have most difficulty in spelling. They may need time to answer this. Record these words. When you have your list of words, try to find words that share a sound or visual pattern. Create a list of 10 common words that seem to be causing the most trouble and share them with your teacher, who will find a way to help your class learn them.

Generally, inquiry questions or investigations could be given once a week or 9 or 10 times a term as a part of spelling word work. I found it was better to allow flexible time for inquiry questions. It is better not to confine work on them to one period or one day, as students seem to enjoy coming up with more words to add to their lists.

Consider, too, the possibility of the class generating its own inquiry question. Devising inquiries or investigations related to spelling patterns makes cognitive demand on intelligence and helps students think about words. It also leads to deeper student engagement and moves students from being bored to being involved, from groaning to growing as writers.

Students I met years after I taught them told me how much they remembered our work together. They remembered how much fun they had investigating questions like these, and, of course, all the writing they did. They also remembered the work we did in drama — I found that to be an interesting combination. Perhaps it was the amount of thinking and problem solving involved in both.

Books of lists are very helpful in these or similar activities. One recommended title is *The Spelling Teacher's Book of Lists* by Jo Phenix (published by Pembroke).

Since many schools now have wireless access to iPads, laptops, or netbooks, it would also be quite appropriate for students to use these digital tools to search for words.

Ongoing Formative Assessment with Descriptive Feedback

Although building word knowledge is important, students need to know how they are progressing. For this to happen, it is helpful for teachers to have simple formative assessments and to team them with descriptive feedback to maximize student success. Just as it is necessary to pay attention to words during investigations and inquiries, so it is necessary for students to pay attention to patterns in words and notice details, record what they wonder about, and ask questions to clarify or probe more deeply into the complexities of language.

The best way of assessing students' spelling knowledge is to confer with them after they have proofread and edited their writing. Doing so would constitute a type of ongoing formative assessment. You could discuss with them strategies they used to find misspelled words and recommend new strategies. You could also address common patterns of error in the class in small groups through discussion, problem solving with words, and short, targeted lessons.

Sometimes, as students build word knowledge, I found, it is helpful to devise short assessment tools related to common problems in written work to maintain the spelling–writing link. The purpose of the assessment would be to give students feedback, so that they could better understand sound patterns and improve their spelling.

For more on descriptive feedback, read *How to Give Effective Feedback to Your Students* by Susan M. Brookhart (Alexandria, VA: Association for Supervision and Curriculum Development, 2008).

If a student or a number of students are having a particular difficulty — for instance, misspelling words with short vowels — they may not be hearing the sounds clearly, may be unaware of multiple sound patterns, or may not be paying attention visually to how the words are formed. I found that a short formative assessment followed by descriptive feedback related to this assessment leads to deeper awareness and greater student success.

Descriptive feedback is a successful strategy, highlighted by Susan Brookhart and others, as a way of helping students learn from the work they are doing and apply this learning to both their current and new work. This strategy works equally well for spelling. It also works across grades and for students of any age.

Assessing understanding of sound patterns

The sample assessment that follows suggests one way to assess student understanding of sound patterns in Grade 3 or 4. In the first assessment, students should be able to read the words, but if they can't read them, simplify the assessment. The assessment is available in linemaster format in the Appendix.

Assessment #1: Short vowels: Sound pattern — Grade 3 or 4
Ask students to read each word below (or other words you have chosen to better suit students' reading abilities). Listen for the vowel sound. Ask students to sort the words into the column where they match the *sound*, not the letter. The top of a sample chart is provided.

> inch, catch, does, quit, buzz
> rock, last, gone, red, picnic
> much, was, swam, plant, splash
> guess, sticky, tall, caught, rest

sound /a/ as in class	sound /e/ as in step	sound /i/ as in tick	sound /o/ as in stop	sound /u/ as in dust

This assessment will show you quickly if students can clearly discriminate sounds in a short list. Students need to be reassured that many words stay true to sound, although there are definitely some exceptions in the patterns.

The descriptive feedback and teachable moment here is that some words have the sound /u/ and use the letter *u* as in *dust*, whereas some words have the sound /u/ but are exceptions and use *oe* as in *does*. These are the words that students need to list and remember. This variation is why the words *was* and *does* are commonly misspelled — students may have an "aha" moment here.

Students need to notice that *guess* has a silent *u* and may want to start a short list of words that have a silent *u*, for example, *guess, guest, guide, guidance,* and *guideline*. To help them understand this anomaly, you may want to share with them that *e* and *i* soften g; hence, the *u* is inserted to harden *g*.

Assessing ability to create lists with patterns

The second assessment is about creating lists with patterns. If students have not done this before, they would need practice in generating lists before they are given the informal assessment. The assessment is available in linemaster format in the Appendix.

Assessment #2: Creating lists related to a sound pattern: Long vowels and vowel combinations — Grades 3 to 5
Ask students to create lists with the same sound and same spelling pattern as the vowels below. The words can rhyme, but do not always need to (e.g., *take* and *taken* under *lake*; *rain* under *fair*). Students would need to have had previous experience in generating lists of words according to sound with the same spelling. They may be able to come up with about five words for each column.

l<u>ake</u>	pl<u>ay</u>	f<u>air</u>

I would tend to co-create an anchor chart with students after each of these assessments, listing what children had learned and what they will now apply to their writing.

Noticing, wondering, questioning

Once students finish a table based on the above, you could ask them to fill out Notice-Wonder-Question responses. Here are some observations by Grade 5 students:

> "I noticed that for *lake*, all my words end in *-ake*."
> "I noticed that all the words have a vowel."
> "I noticed that some words like *mayor* sound like it's *ai*, but it's not."

> "I wonder why *liar* and *lair* sound different, but are almost spelled the same."
> "I wonder if 'jay' is a word."
> "I wonder why there are so many words that rhyme."
> "I wonder if there is more than 1000 of these words."
> "I wonder if *ay* is at the end of these words all the time."
> "I wonder if there was any word that didn't quite have anything to match it."
> "I wonder how many words have *ake*, *ay*, or *ai* in them."

> "My question is, why do words not rhyme but have the same pattern like *clay* and *layers*?"
> "My question is, why could *paid* go in the *ai* column, but not *said*?"
> "My question is, why are there so many words that rhyme with *fair*?"

These questions and comments could lead to some interesting discussions and renew the quest to learn more, know more, and think more about words.

Modifying the activity: Two patterns only

If students have difficulty with this activity, it would be good to take them back to generating just two patterns, instead of three, and then have them look at the words and record what they notice about these two patterns. You could model doing this, for example, demonstrating how to come up with *oi* and *oy* words: by thinking of rhymes (e.g., *boil, foil, coil, soil* for *oi*, and *boy, toy, coy, joy* for *oy*) and by thinking of the sound at the beginning (e.g., *oil, oink, oilcan, oilcloth, oily, ointment,* and *oyster*). Be sure to ask students which strategy they use to create lists of words and have them share.

Sample activity: Create a list of words for the sound /oi/ as in *foil* and for /oy/ as in *boy*.

/oi/ as in foil		/oy/ as in boy	
coil	join	coy	joy
spoil	android	toy	Ahoy!
asteroid	avoid	annoy	convoy
oil	broil	destroy	enjoy
toilet	moist	employ	cowboy

The Notice-Wonder strategy could be used as a way for students to respond as they observe these lists of words. You could then provide descriptive feedback, as in the sample comment shown in the margin. Here are some Notice comments from students:

> "I noticed that *l* and *n* are common endings in the *oi* section."
> "I noticed that *oi* is in the middle of most words."
> "I noticed that *oy* is at the end of most words."
> "I noticed that there are not a lot of words in the Canadian language that start with *oi* or *oy*."
> "I noticed that most (not all) *oy* words are at the end, and *oi* is almost always in the middle."
> "I noticed that some words like *voyage* had *oy* in the middle."
> "I noticed that some words are totally written different, like *royal* and *foil*."

Descriptive Feedback: Example

Teacher feedback on student observations is usually oral. If, for example, you heard comments such as those here, you might say, "Using *oy* at the end of a word holds true most of the time, unless you add to a base word. *Employ* is an example, but it would be *employs* and *employed*. *Annoy* is another example, and then it would be *annoys, annoyed,* and *annoying.* The word *oyster* starts with *oy,* but it is pretty much the only word. But you're right. If you hear the sound /oy/ at the end of a word, you usually spell it *oy.*"

If the students are unsure of how to respond, I would model the observation "I noticed that on my list, the sound /oy/ usually comes at the end of words and /oi/ seems to come before the end." I would then make a wonder statement: "I wonder if this is true for most /oy/ words . . ." Instead of a Notice-Wonder-Question structure, you could keep with the simpler Notice-Wonder structure and continue to model and provide guided practice until students can respond independently. Some students, I find, prefer Notice-Wonder or Notice-Question, but some are comfortable with all three components, if given clear explanations and practice. When they use this structure, students begin to pay attention to words in remarkable detail and to ask better questions over time.

Assessing awareness of long vowel patterns

Students would be asked to read each word listed below and then listen for the vowel sound. Alternatively, you could modify the word list to better suit the reading ability of students, keeping in mind that there should be several exceptions, but not too many. Students are to sort the words into the column where they match visual patterns and the vowel sound: *played* and *day* match, for example, but *light* and *site* do not. This activity appears in linemaster format in the Appendix.

Assessment #3: Sorting by visual and sound pattern: Long vowels — Grade 4 or 5

say, care, great, always
seat, fair, said, main
hair, chairs, reed, tray
leap, need, kayak, beat
deed, peak, may, feed

Long /a/ as in *day*	Long /a/ as in *rain*	Long /e/ as in *eat*	Long /e/ as in *seed*	Words that don't match
say	hair	seat	deed	care
may	fair	leap	need	great
always	chairs	peak	reed	said
tray	main	beat	feed	kayak

This sorting would give students information about regular patterns, as well as other patterns that they need to note and remember. If you use the Notice-Wonder strategy to record their thinking, perhaps one student would point out that *care* has another long /a/ pattern, which involves words that have long *a* and end in *e*. If not, you may arrange for students to discover this in a further investigation of vowel sounds.

Here are some student comments in response to doing this activity:

"I noticed that the words that don't match kinda fooled your brain, because they are kinda spelled the same."
"I noticed that *great* was not supposed to go under long *a* as in *day*."
"I noticed that the words look the same, but they don't sound the same at all."
"I noticed that the words that were left out kind of look like they go in some columns, but sound different."

Initially, it is enough for students just to pay attention and notice how word patterns work; they can move on to wondering about words and composing questions about them later on.

The next activity would also deal with long vowels. Here is a recommended inquiry question:

Inquiry: Do more words have *ay*, *ey*, or *oy*? What do you predict? Make a table to generate lists.

There are more than 1200 words containing *ay*, at least 700 with *ey*, and at least 500 with *oy*. It would be interesting to see how this is reflected in the students' lists. It is unlikely that they will come close to these numbers, which is just fine.

long /a/ sound as *ay*	long /e/ sound as *ey*	long /o/ sound in *oy*
bay	monkey	annoy

Long vowel patterns for future word generation could be as follows:
ai, ay, a_e, ee, ea, ei, ie, ey, i_e, oa, oy, ow, ou, oi, ui, u_e, uy, ue [guess].

Conducting this informal assessment will give you a sense if students have learned something about patterns in words, particularly long vowel patterns. Have them make notes for future editing and to foster their awareness of words and patterns. Students can be made aware of certain sound patterns and generate words both before and after assessment, as practice is important.

One way to provide constructive feedback

If the teacher has noticed that a student has frequent problems with exceptions to the short /o/ sound, he might direct the student or a small group to list some words with regular short /o/ sounds from their writing, then ask the students to to list exceptions and build patterns. Over time, their list might look something like the one following. The teacher's feedback would be to assist the students in using the lists as they edit.

sound /o/ (regular)	words with sound /o/ with other words in their pattern (irregular)
soft	wasp, want
gone	caught, taught, haughty, jaunt
lock	talk, walk, chalk, stalk

For students beyond Grade 3, I have referred to personal dictionaries as "lexical dictionaries," as a way to involve the students in exploring vocabulary and in further stimulating their interest in words.

Words listed in this way are helpful to students only if the words are used in writing, and if the students refer to the lists constantly and add to them. A personal dictionary, used for recording lists like these, can become a discussion point, and in writer's workshop, new findings can be shared, checked, and used in editing. Use of a personal dictionary can go on throughout the grades, as words become more complex.

Mastering vowels and their exceptions is some of the most complex word work students can do, and it always takes longer than you think! Although there can be mini-lessons to build word knowledge, work in isolation is rarely applied to writing. Much more successful is cognitive understanding of sound patterns, a growing knowledge of the multiple and varied combinations, and the memorization or making of notes on exceptions. When students are learning to spell in these ways, they are truly developing spelling consciousness.

Application: The Heart of the Matter

When students have worked on creating words in lists related to sound, they can apply what they now know in many ways. Here are three ways to make application explicit. These ways will help some but not all students; however, teachers can use these approaches to give feedback.

1. Know-Share-Use

Students can share with a partner, in a group, or with the whole class, using this strategy Know-Share-Use (or portions of it).

Student sample A
KNOW — I know that *was* and *does* don't spell as they sound.
SHARE — I will share this with my group.

Student sample B
KNOW — I know that if I hear the sound /oi/ at the end of a word, I will spell it *oy*.
USE — I will check for this when I edit.

A teacher applying this strategy might say to a student:
KNOW — You know that you need to look at visual patterns as well as sound patterns — *said* and *because* are words you should check.
USE — You need to list these two words, and use them to check when you edit your work.

2. Visual checking, or does it look right?

After working with words and patterns, students develop a visual sense of what looks right. They learn numerous patterns and alternatives for different sounds, so if one word does not look right, they try the other spelling of that sound. If a child wanted to write *play* but was unsure of how to do it, he could try *ai* and *ay*, writing "plai" and *play* and choosing one of them.

You could adopt visual checking as a group practice activity. Begin by writing a pair of words on the board and asking the students to record the word they believe to be correct. Offer immediate feedback. Students could self-check and make a note of words about which they are unsure. Build the list pair by pair, as below.

oi as in j**oi**n	**oy** as in b**oy**
✓ coil	coyl

This is the first time for feedback.

oi as in j**oi**n	**oy** as in b**oy**
✓ coil	coyl
joi	✓ joy

The list builds.

oi as in j**oi**n	**oy** as in b**oy**
✓ coil	coyl
joi	✓ joy
✓ coil	oyl

The activity continues. There is only one list, adding one pair at a time.

This activity should probably not have more than 5 to 10 pairs, as it is meant to demonstrate a strategy and allow for practice in visual checking. Immediately after this activity, the misspelled words should be removed from the chalkboard, whiteboard, or SMART Board to avoid the risk of students remembering the wrong spelling.

This strategy is more helpful when used by individual students unsure of the spelling, but once in a while, it allows the teacher to assess informally as students try to visually identify the correct spelling. If the teacher or student chooses a pattern (ai, a_e), where a pair of homophones are present (e.g., *pail*, *pale*; *stair*, *stare*), then both words would be spelled correctly. The students would need to check meaning, so that they used the correct word and the correct spelling for that particular meaning.

3. Look-Think-Need

Another three-word strategy related to application is Look-Think-Need. This strategy would have to be taught through modeled and guided practice until students become independent. It deals with metacognition, with students identifying their own needs, so it is well worth the effort.

The teacher displays a piece of writing through document camera, on SMART Board, on overhead projector, or on chart paper, and to model, says something like this:

> LOOK — "I looked at this piece of writing."
> THINK — "I think this student is having trouble with long vowel sounds."
> NEED — "This student needs some help. Can you identify what this student is having trouble with, or can you offer suggestions to help with long vowel sounds?"

There would be discussion in pairs, followed by sharing aloud. A basic student frame is as follows:

> LOOK — "I looked at my latest piece of writing."
> THINK — "I think I am having trouble with . . ."

Or

> LOOK — "I looked over my work to edit it."
> NEED — "I need help with . . ."

After teacher modeling and lots of time to practise, a student might be able to complete the frame much like this:

> LOOK — "I looked at my latest piece of writing."
> THINK — "I think I am having trouble with . . . vowel pairs."

Or

> LOOK — "I looked over my work to edit it."
> NEED — "I need help with . . . vowel pairs, because that's where I make most mistakes."

Author Patricia Cunningham expands on this strategy in *What Really Matters in Spelling?*

The Think comment would refer to a piece of writing from a student from a previous class. No name would be showing. Alternatively, it could be a piece the teacher devised to address a common problem.

This expressed need, which has encouraged students to self-assess, could lead to a series of mini-lessons on vowel pairs, followed by investigation into vowel pairs in tables, as shown previously. It is unlikely that a single student would be the only one having issues with vowel pairs, but the student who filled this frame would be more motivated to join a group learning about this due to self-identification of the problem. Initially, it will be more common for students to identify words that are causing them trouble than matters such as vowel pairs. The teacher will be able to see connections (e.g., most commonly misspelled words, sound patterns, or vowel pairs).

The role of the teacher is to move students along the continuum from words with single vowels (e.g., *cat, mist*) to words with vowel pairs or groups (e.g., *peak, maid, beauty*). So, the teacher works to strike the balance between having students investigate, inquire, and ask questions on the one hand, and helping them build word knowledge on the other. The teacher must always remember that the goal is to bring students closer and closer to making more accurate spelling predictions as they write. An informed prediction is so much better than a wild guess, and a growing spelling consciousness helps to inform these predictions.

3

Building Word Knowledge: An Ongoing Strategy

Although some knowledge of sound is ongoing, the next phase of learning is the building of *syntactic* knowledge, so that students know more about the structure of words, base words, and how words change as inflectional endings are added, as they become plurals, or as they are compounded.

Students would begin to progress along this chart to focus on syntactic knowledge or function patterns.

less difficult ⟶ more difficult

Graphophonic Knowledge	Syntactic Knowledge	Semantic Knowledge
sound and visual appearance of words	grammatical function and syntax of words	meaning and origin of words

This chart provides more detail on what students need to know, mapping the progression. It could be used for planning.

Pattern by Sound/ Visual Appearance (Graphophonic)	Pattern by Function (Syntactic)	Pattern by Meaning (Semantic)
the knowledge that the alphabet names stay constant, but the sounds change	base words	wordplay (e.g., puns, riddles, jokes)
consonant sounds	verb endings (e.g., *-ed*, *-ing*)	prefixes (as they relate to base words)
short vowel patterns	plurals	suffixes (as they relate to base words)
long vowel patterns	contractions	word origins
vowel pairs with choices (e.g., *oi* or *oy* — *oy* is usually at the end of words)	compound words (hyphen or no hyphen; separate or together?)	word narratives related to word origins
silent letters related to letters that have sound (e.g., *crum**b***, *crum**ble***)	adjectives	idioms
vowels plus *r*	adverbs	similes, metaphors

It cannot be emphasized enough that this information is to help the teacher, as she perceives student needs in their written work and decides to address them through mini-lessons and group work. Once students recognize a perceived need, they are more likely to see relevance in word work.

Base Word Basics

Please feel free to create other short chants or alternative versions with your students, or to use other points of engagement.

Building word knowledge without causing boredom is a challenge, so I have introduced chants to create novelty, to which the brain responds, as a welcome diversion from developing innumerable word lists. I found initially that students were surprised when I used chants, as they tended to associate chants with choral speaking in a drama lesson, not a spelling lesson; however, once they were able to read them in a variety of ways — softly, in deep voices, with the text divided into two groups, with the text divided into pairs and solo voices — they broadened their view of chants and participated well. Engagement is always important.

> **Bases Loaded**
> A base word stands on its own.
> A suffix comes at the end.
> So *swim* becomes *swimming*,
> *Run* becomes *running* —
> Starting the trend.
> A base word stands on its own
> A prefix comes before it.
> So, *known* becomes *unknown*,
> *Spell* becomes *misspell* —
> You can explore it!

This chant can be used to introduce the concept of base words, and a baseball game, as described below, can follow to involve students in adding the inflectional ending *-ing* to a base word. At home base, students can take this further, and if they do, the words need to have two *regular* endings, for example, *skip*, *skipping*, and *skipped*, but not *run*, *running*, and *ran*.

Base Word Baseball: Directions

1. To accommodate this game, desks and tables need to be moved to the centre or the perimeter of the room.
2. The students are divided into two teams. There are three bases marked by colored beanbags or small flags, and a nerf ball is used as a baseball. The ball can be hit by hand or by a small table-tennis bat.
3. One team is up to bat. Students have three tries to hit the ball. One catch puts the team out.
4. The opposing team contributes a pitcher, a person at each of the three bases, and a backstop. There are only two people in outfield (at the back of the room), and the other team members are observers. Only the base players, the backstop, and the pitcher can put someone out.
5. The teacher calls out a base word. The pitcher throws the ball, and the batter hits the ball. *Before* the batter gets to first base, the student needs to call out an affix (prefix or suffix) for this base word. (For example, if the teacher calls, *"Prod,"* the student calls, *"Prodding."*) If the student is unable to provide an affix, she or he is out. *After* a student has reached all three bases and made

it back to home base, the student is given a point for a home run. When the team strikes out, the other team goes up to bat. Points are awarded for every correct affix and every home run. The team with the most points wins.

6. The teacher can referee until she feels that someone has the maturity to take on the role; she can delegate refereeing responsibilities once the class has played a few times.

When I taught in Windsor, Ontario, this "baseball game" was played over and over in my class with all kinds of variations, depending on what I was reviewing. The students never tired of playing, perhaps because the game involved movement and had a competitive edge, and because they often had choice in what they reviewed.

Inflectional Endings and Double Consonants

After you have introduced the concept of base words, students need to know that all words are not straightforward. When they add -*ing* to *running*, for example, it involves doubling a letter. This happens to many, but not all words, but it causes a problem in spelling and needs to be addressed.

Students need to focus on "looking for double letters" in their writing at the ends of words, as they continue to build knowledge about words and editing. They need to notice double letters as they create words with them and as they check for how accurately they use them through editing.

Reading this poem chorally may help introduce and reinforce key ideas about double consonants.

> **Double or Nothing!**
> In a pattern of consonant, short vowel, consonant,
> Sometimes known as C, V, C,
> Double the last letter, then add -*ing* or *e, d*.
> Then *stop* becomes *stopped* or *stopping*
> And *hop* becomes *hopped* or *hopping*.
> But don't think of doubling,
> If the word ends in *e*:
> *Rake* becomes *raked* or *raking*.
> *Fake* becomes *faked* or *faking*.
> **Double for C V C —**
> **But *not* if the word ends in *e*.**

As soon as students read this chant aloud, encourage them to test it out, to verify through inquiry what it says about doubling consonants. You might ask them: "Explain the difference between *hop* and *hopping*, *hope* and *hoping*. Does the rule 'Double for C V C' help you or not?" (It promises only 80 percent accuracy.)

You could create a three-column table, such as the one started on the next page, so that students can practise adding -*ed* and -*ing* endings to base words before looking at their latest piece of writing for words that end in -*ed* or -*ing*. They will need to consider that the last letter in the base word may — or may not — need doubling.

base word	-ed ending	-ing ending
stop		
crop		
rake		

Other words to add to a list include *fake, shop, rob, mob, smoke,* and *hope.*

Applying use of double consonants with word endings to writing

It will be interesting to observe whether students can find words on their own, whether they need to work in pairs, or whether they need the teacher to model, using a short student sample, such as the one below:

> The young man *changed* after the old lady told him not to boss people around. So he **choped** down his tower and <u>gave</u> other people his sticks to help build a shcool and a house.

Here, one ending is correct and one is not. Students could suggest which one is correct and why, then determine how to fix the one that is incorrect. Further proofreading could reveal that the student has one other spelling mistake, but all the letters are there. The teacher could also note that the writer used *gave* correctly and did not write "gived."

Here is another sample where students could decide whether the Grade 3 student has spelled both italicized words correctly, and explain why they think that.

> I can apply the author's lesson by *stopping* and *using* my brain.

You would expect students to say that these are two different endings. In *stopping,* the student is doubling and then adding *-ing* to the base word, but in *using,* she dropped the *e* before adding *-ing.* Students need practice at explaining before they can do this, I found, so this sample could serve as a teacher model. The rule "Double for C V C — but *not* if the word ends in *e*" is easy to remember and may help some students to edit as well as to explain, because thinking about words is always the goal.

Most words with a C V C pattern will double the final consonants, but there are exceptions students should note. Suggest that they keep these lists in a Writer's notebook. Or, they could list them in a Word and Phrase Collection book, where interesting words and phrases are noted from mentor texts (model texts that the students have read), as well as spelling exceptions.

When students have completed their initial investigations and begun to edit by looking for *-ed* and *-ing* endings in their own writing, consider having a group or class discussion on the fact that the rule — "Double for C V C — but *not* if the word ends in *e*" — does not cover all examples. Interest in words is what we want to engender, and if students are finding too many exceptions, a good discussion could develop around the question "Should we scrap this rule — does it work for us?"

Extending the rule could be an option, but the big question to ask students is this: "Does the rule work for you?"

Double for C V C —
But *not* if the word ends in *e*
And *not* if the word ends V V C.

V V C means vowel-vowel-consonant, as in *cheer*, which becomes *cheered* or *cheering*. Now, with more information, students may need a chance to practise in a sample table to get used to these words, or they could directly edit their writing for these endings. Below is the start of a table for adding suffixes correctly. Other good words to include in the left column are *cap, jar, bake, rain, cheat, drain,* and *lap*.

base word	*-ed* ending	*-ing* ending
cheer		
wait		
cheat		

Further questions will arise, so you may want to set students off investigating or consolidate findings for those who already have this information. Writing a chant would be a worthwhile student activity, as students have to remember what they learned about *-ing* and *-ed*. The shorter the rhyme, the easier it is to remember. The rhymes could be shared, and students could take part in thoughtful discussion about what helps them as they check word endings while editing.

During one such discussion, students told me that they had just realized that "t" was not usually an ending; they had relied on sound, as in "walkt" or "stopt," but now they were adding *-ed* and making fewer errors. Other students told me that they had been leaving the *-e* when adding *-ing*, and now they were taking the *e* off first. One student said that, "Drop the *e; add i n g*" was a rhyme that helped her remember what to do.

Before we began to look at endings, a number of students said they felt that everything was random and without pattern. Enabling students to edit by knowing what works is a way to foster independence and allow them to be more successful at peer- and self-editing.

<aside>Note that *focused* used to have a double *s*, but now it most often does not. Students need to be made aware that language and spelling change over time and also that different countries have different spellings of some words.</aside>

Some information on *c, h, q, w, x,* and *y*, related to doubling

When words end in the italicized letters noted above, they usually do not double. An interesting exercise would be to have students search for words where *-ed* and *-ing* are added to words ending with these letters. They can work alone or in pairs and choose two or three of the letters to search. The idea here is to explore and identify how words work, and determine whether these letters have something in common at the end of words, or not. It may take students some time, but they will likely find the following:

c Base words ending in *c*, add *k* before the verb ending. The reason for this is that "*i* softens *c*," and *c* needs to have a hard sound here.	mimic, mimicked, mimicking picnic, picnicked, picnicking panic, panicked, panicking

H	
If *h* is at the end of a verb, it is never doubled. Few verbs in English have double *h* (e.g., *withhold, hitchhike*). Students tend to add *-ed* to the base word, so these words are rarely a problem, except that students want to insert an extra *t* in *attach*.	watch, watched, watching hatch, hatched, hatching attach, attached, attaching dash, dashed, dashing fish, fished, fishing brush, brushed, brushing
W	
Few words have two *w*'s, so they look unusual (e.g., *bowwow, glowworm, powwow*). They do not double before an ending. Students may want to generate a much longer list to see whether this continues to work, or to note past tense exceptions, such as *know, knew, knowing; grow, grew, growing*. They may also have fun playing with the words and creating sentences. For example: The glowworms at the powwow created interesting lighting effects.	flow, flowed, flowing glow, glowed, glowing allow, allowed, allowing bellow, bellowed, bellowing caw, cawed, cawing chew, chewed, chewing powwow, powwowed, powwowing
X	
Virtually no words in English have *xx* (except for the company name *Exxon*); *x* is never doubled before adding an ending.	fax, faxed, faxing fix, fixed, fixing box, boxed, boxing flex, flexed, flexing relax, relaxed, relaxing wax, waxed, waxing tax, taxed, taxing vex, vexed, vexing
Y	
Past tense changes some words that end in *y*: *say, said, saying; fly, flew, flying; buy, bought, buying*. If the word ends with a consonant before the *y*, change *y* to *i* and add *ed* for past tense, but that's all (e.g., *cry, cried, crying; apply, applied, applying; try, tried, trying*).	stay, stayed, staying play, played, playing enjoy, enjoyed, enjoying betray, betrayed, betraying decay, decayed, decaying fray, frayed, fraying pray, prayed, praying spray, sprayed, spraying

Three common choices

As students explore endings further, or cycle back to them at a later date, the information in the following chant may help them in their editing search to find and correct verb endings.

> **Verb Endings**
> When you alter the tense of most verbs,
> Three simple strategies work.
> You add *e* and *d* to most words.
> So *want* becomes *wanted*,
> And *work* becomes *worked*.

D is the next common ending.
Add *d* if the verb ends in *e*,
So you change *use* to *used*,
And you change *fuse* to *fused*
By adding that one letter *d*.
The last change turns *y* to *i*
And again, you add *e* and *d*.
So *carry* becomes *carried*,
And *marry* becomes *married*.
As you write, these three choices are key.

This chant serves to simplify the search for endings by outlining three choices: (1) adding *ed*, (2) adding *d*, and (3) changing *y* to *i* before adding *ed*.

Based on this, students should be able to edit their own work for these three endings, and then self-correct and check. Knowing the rules makes the editing doable, as students build their word knowledge. Encourage them to list exceptions in their Writer's notebook, Word and Phrase Collection book, a notebook you assign to record what they are learning about words, or on an iPad or tablet.

Some students may soon be ready to look for both double letters and verb endings. They may prefer to work in pairs to do this. Keep in mind that even if you have had much practice editing, editing work for every error is complex. A vast bank of word knowledge, a growing knowledge of exceptions, and, of course, an ever increasing base of new words are required. Since the students need the practice more than we do, we must be sure to give them the tools and let them go ahead. Students will become better with practice, perhaps even expert in certain areas, as they engage with words and notice more each day about how words work.

Editing Towards Independence

So far in this book, the editing strategies that have been suggested can be summed up in a student checklist as follows:

I can edit by . . .
creating lists of visual and sound patterns
creating a growing list of exceptions for use when editing
checking for words with double consonants
checking verb endings

The strategies are based on building word knowledge and increasing awareness of spelling patterns. As students use certain strategies successfully, they can check the boxes, which will help them feel that they are in charge of their work.

There will have to be ongoing discussions as a class, in small groups, and in pairs about what students notice as they are editing and learning more about how words work. You can give them feedback on how their editing is improving and how they can improve further. Perhaps certain students always forget to check verb endings. They may be able to reread a chant and just check their writing for that one item. Doing this will build their confidence as editors. As always, the goal is to help them edit independently and become proficient over time.

Structure of Words: Riddles

As a break from looking directly at word structure — for example, consonant doubling — you can adopt an indirect way of encouraging your students to focus on word structure: generating riddles. Riddles, such as the following, help students to become aware of smaller words within words.

Riddles for inquiry into word structure

Find two words containing commonly known trees, for example, *fir* is in *first*.
(*Examples:* **d**ash, s**oak**, al**pine**)

Find three or more words containing the word *is*.
(*Examples:* h**is**, th**is**, l**is**t, m**is**t, f**is**t)

Find the animal in **tape** and the insect in **pants**; then, create an animal riddle like this for someone else to solve.

If you find a bird in *bowl*, what animal would you find in *catch*? Can you think of others?
(*Examples:* **rat**e, **shrew**d)

These riddles are quite straightforward, but they focus attention on word structure and awareness, and students may wish to create more complex riddles. These activities should be ongoing to make students more aware of the structure of words. Here are examples of more complex riddles, created by students:

Find three words with a part of a shark and three words with a body part.
(*Examples:* **fin**ish, **fin**e, con**fin**e, de**fin**e, **fin**ger; h**ear**th, **eye**lid, monk**eye**d)
Find three words with the contents of a pen and three words with the end of a fish.
(*Examples:* **ink**, r**ink**, s**ink**, shr**ink**; de**tail**, **tail**or, pony**tail**, re**tail**)

Find four words containing something you write with and two words with the part of a ship that is moved by the wind.
(*Examples:* **pen**cil, o**pen**, car**pen**ter, dee**pen**, hap**pen**, shar**pen**; **sail**or, **sail**boat, **sail**ing, **sail**s)

Once students have seen a few models for these types of riddles, they should be able to create riddles of their own to challenge a partner or someone in their small group.

Vowels pose an interesting challenge.

> For each of the five vowels, can you find a word that doubles the vowel —
> for example, *aardvark* or *feel*?
> (*Examples:* baa, aardvark, naan, bazaar; eel; skiing, taxiing, radii, Hawaii;
> moon; vacuum, continuum)
> I listed extra words as answers for *aa*, *ii*, and *uu*, as they are uncommon
> spellings.

> How many words can you find with three *a*'s in them?
> (*Examples:* banana, alpaca, barracuda, bandanna, rutabaga, Canada,
> Canadian, Dalmatian, Guatemala, Australia, Malaysia, tarantula, Himalayas,
> Panama, apparatus)

> How many words can you find with three *e*'s in them?
> (*Examples:* beetle, breeze, centipede, deeper, degrees, expensive, needed,
> needle, preteen, screened, seventeen, severe, sneeze, sweeter, telephone,
> tweeter, tweezers)

> How many words can you find with three *i*'s in them?
> (You will either need to provide clues or perhaps you can change the question to two *i*'s.)
> (*Examples:* bikini, civilian, civilize, dividing, idiotic, initial, infinity,
> mimicking, significant)

> Can you find more words with consecutive double letters? Try to include
> one double vowel, as in *raccoon*.
> (*Examples:* balloon, tattoo, committee, Tennessee, bookkeeper)

> Two words in English end in -*gry*. One is *angry*. What is the other one?
> (Hungry.)

I found that when students involved their families in finding the second -*gry* word, they seemed to really enjoy this riddle. Parents were also impressed that students knew about the obsolete word *puggry*.

Presenting a New Challenge — the Endings -*er*, -*or*, and -*ar*

We have looked at creating chants to provide novelty and riddles to involve wordplay. Now we will look at cognitive challenge: creating an inquiry around specific word endings. Initially, the teacher would suggest such an inquiry, but the intention is that students develop a spirit of inquiry and engage in asking questions and investigating their answers together. Such a community of learners would wonder about words and ask questions related to how words work.

There used to be many more English words with the -*gry* ending, but they have become obsolete. The puzzle often asks for a third word. The third word, a word we no longer use, is *puggry*. It means a scarf worn around a sun helmet. Even more interesting: There are three alternative spellings for this word — *pugree*, *puggree*, and *puggaree*! Another obsolete word for hungry, *anhungry*, remains in some dictionaries because it is quoted in Shakespeare's *Coriolanus*, Act 1.

Inquiry: Predict whether more people have jobs ending in *or* (*author*) or *er* (*writer*). Create lists to find out whether your prediction was correct. Which was most common, or were the lists similar in length? Consider leaving your two lists as a classroom chart for reference. You may add more words as you discover them.

Students who are on their way to knowing much about words may find it interesting to note that *writer* ends in -*er*, but *author, editor,* and *illustrator* end in -*or*. Beyond that, *author,* although it has the same ending as *illustrator* and *editor,* does not have a base word; the other two words do.

Note that more than 10 times as many words end in -*er* than in -*or* and -*ar* put together. So students need to know that they have more chance of being correct if they use -*er* as an ending. -*er* is also the most common ending referring to someone who is doing something, for example, a baker, a writer.

In my experience, once given two or three sample words, students never seem to tire of creating word lists like these. Your students can do the same. I have included the base, or root, word here for clarity.

write	writer	teach	teacher
fight	fighter	dance	dancer
print	printer	drive	driver
clean	cleaner	manage	manager
wash	washer	play	player
bake	baker	swim	swimmer
intrude	intruder	travel	traveler
bank	banker	advertise	advertiser

Words ending in -*or* are the next most common, something that would be determined by student investigation, but students may find out or need to be guided to explore that -*or* tends to use certain endings on base words: -*ct*, -*ate*, and -*it*.

-ct	-ate	-it
conduct — conductor	create — creator	visit — visitor
contract — contractor	investigate — investigator	edit — editor
compact — compactor	calculate — calculator	inhibit — inhibitor
predict — predictor	delegate — delegator	deposit — depositor
act — actor	regulate — regulator	exhibit — exhibitor
	accelerate — accelerator	
	calibrate — calibrator	
	cultivate — cultivator	
	illustrate — illustrator	

Exploring less common word endings

The five words all finish with the letters *lar*.

Inquiry: Even fewer words end in *-ar* than end in *-or*. Notice that these five words — *popular, similar, pillar, regular, cellar* — all have something in common. What is it? Does this pattern hold true for other *-ar* words? How many can you find?

Answer: *Dollar, burglar, caterpillar, collar, molar, exemplar, scholar, particular, pedlar, angular, solar, circular, stellar, spectacular, poplar,* and *polar* all end in *-lar*; however, *vicar, grammar, calendar,* and *altar* do not — have students remember these four words.

This exploration of endings may result in students writing a verse similar to this one. The subject matter can vary, but the focus should be on the structure of words.

> Although a writer writes,
> An author does not auth,
> An editor will edit,
> But a mother does not moth.
> Although a baker bakes,
> A tailor never tails,
> A doctor will not doct,
> But a sailor always sails.

Over my years teaching, I have found that, while students may dislike editing and feel ambivalent towards spelling, they are often fascinated by the structure and variance in words. For that reason, I know that they will find it engaging to create or co-create other verses to this short chant. You may want to check out the work of Richard Lederer, who has written many rhymes similar to this one. One of his books, *Crazy English*, looks at the anomalies of the English language with wit and wisdom.

An evolving checklist for editing

We are now adding to student word knowledge, so their editing checklist is increasing and, it is hoped, their ability to create a growing list of items for it. Here is a sample checklist with a focus on some word endings.

I edit by . . .	Check off what you are looking for in your writing	Teacher's Comments
checking words with double consonants for inflectional endings (*-ing, -ed*) • doubles if word ends c v c • does not double if word ends in *e* • does not double if word ends v v c		

checking verb endings (-ed, -d; change y to i and add -ed)		
looking for endings -er, -or, -ar; remembering -er is the most common		

After conferring with the students or a group of students, the teacher may add certain editing items by writing in blanks on a checklist, or the students may collaborate with the teacher to identify common problems, which could lead to a mini-lesson with a group of students.

Shunning "Shun"

Once, when I was teaching full time, I decided to address a problem my Grade 4 students were having with the ending sound /shun/. They were misspelling it in a variety of ways, but the most common misspelling was "shun." I checked, and the ending /shun/ is **never** spelled that way. After further checking, I found that 1200 words end in -ation. So I told my students this and asked them to find a few. I was hoping that this would be a warm-up activity lasting 10 to 15 minutes; instead, the work lasted for 10 to 15 days. We covered multiple sheets of chart paper with lengthy lists, and just when I thought we were finished, they would approach me during yard duty and say, "I have another word — *designation*." "I have another word — *navigation*." I think their goal was to reach 1200! The good news was that no one ever wrote "shun" at the end of a word again.

The students also created chants, as in the example below. With chants, the possibilities are endless, and for transitions to other classes, or when lining up for gym, students can gain a little extra practice in spelling, while having fun with words.

> **Chant for *a-tion***
> A, t, i, o, n; a, t, i, o, n,
> Spells *a-tion*,
> Give me an *n*.
> What does it say?
> Nation.
> N . . . a, t, i, o, n,
> Nation.
>
> Give me an *s* and a *t*.
> What does it say?
> Station.
> S, t . . . a, t, i, o, n,
> Station.
> Give me a *v*, *a*, *c*.
> What does it say?
> Vacation.
> V, a, c . . . a, t, i, o, n,
> vacation.

Give me a *d, o, n.*
What does it say?
Donation,
d, o, n . . . a, t, i, o, n,
Donation.
Give me an *l, o, c.*
What does it say?
Location.
L, o, c . . . a, t, i, o, n
Location.

a, t, i,o, n; a, t, i, o, n,
Spells *a-tion.*

To continue having fun with words, this chant may engage your students when they look at words ending with the sound /shun/. I am sure they would enjoy substituting their own choice of words ending in *-tion* or *-ation*, or they may just want to co-create their own verse.

Endings
When you hear the sound /shun/
At the end of a word,
Never ever use *s, h, u, n* —
That's preferred!
Most often that sound
Is spelled *t, i, o, n.*
Like *nation* and *station,*
Creation, quotation,
Addition, subtraction
and *multiplication.*

If students choose *-tion* at the end of a word, they will be correct 88 percent of the time. The four exceptions to the *-ation* rule are *Dalmatian, Appalachian, Eustachian,* and *crustacean,* but these are not common words.

Students may also be interested to know that there seems to be a link between words ending in *-ation* and words ending in *-or.* Have them check this out. They may develop a list that looks something like this.

evaluation	evaluator	innovation	innovator
motivation	motivator	simulation	simulator
estimation	estimator	location	locator
education	educator		

Beyond finding out about the *-ation/-or* connection, students may be interested to know that there are other *-or* words that have a connection with words that end not in *-ation,* but with a variation on that. Students may want to develop a new list just to see how many different endings there are. Some results appear in the right column below. This list is a more challenging one to create.

collector	colle**ction**
objector	obje**ction**

professor	profe**ssion**
confessor	confe**ssion**
rejector	reje**ction**
inspector	inspe**ction**
conductor	condu**ction**
reflector	refle**ction**
projector	proje**ction**
exhibitor	exhibi**tion**

The different endings they will find would be *-tion*, *-ction*, and *-ssion*.

While they are looking at alternative spellings for the sound /*shun*/, students may be interested in checking out words that fall into the 12 percent, while *-tion* takes 88 percent. Here are some simple related inquiries.

Sounding like /shun/

1. Find one word that ends in *-shion*.
   (fashion, cushion)
2. Find two words that end in *-cean*.
   (ocean, crustacean) Students may need clues (e.g., a body of salty water; lobsters, crabs, and shrimp belong to this group).
3. Find two words ending in *-cian* that refer to jobs.
   (musician, dietician, politician, statistician) The job angle may help students remember the spelling of these words.
4. Find one word that ends in *-tian* and one that ends in *–sian*, both referring to a nationality.
   (*-tian*, as in Egyptian and Haitian; *-sian*, as in Asian, Malaysian, and Indonesian)

Despite such exceptions, it is good to know that most of the time, the sound /shun/ is spelled *-tion*. As students use words in their writing that are exceptions, encourage them to share what they are learning with others in their group and record this in their Writer's notebook. I found it was helpful if they shared with others in the class:

> **Students share . . .**
> I was writing "television" today, and I noticed it had "sion" at the end. I listed it with "division" in my Writer's notebook.
> I was writing "ocean" today and I noticed it did not match anything I know, so I noted it with exceptions to "tion."

Committing to memory the exceptions that students plan to use is a helpful exercise; otherwise, have them make a note of words ending in *-tion* that interest them.

Adapting editing checklists for student use

When you have finished teaching a mini-lesson or whole-group lesson to increase word knowledge, it can be useful to have students apply it directly to their writing. The editing checklist for that day may look like this:

I can edit by...		
Focus	Student Comment	Teacher Comment
checking for -tion words, including -ation (multiplication) and -ection (selection)		

Students should list exceptions in a Writer's notebook, or on an iPad or tablet, only if they have used or think they will use the words in their writing.

The editing checklist is now adapting to student need. It is ideally short, unless the teacher is having a writing conference with a student and wants to review what the student has learned to apply in editing over several weeks. In that case, the editing list would be longer. It may look like much like the list illustrated below, but it could be either created by the teacher or co-created by the teacher and student to reflect what had been taught and applied — it is important for it to meet students' needs when they edit:

I can edit by...	Checked
creating and/or answering inquiry questions related to word patterns	
checking for words with double letters	
checking verb endings: -ed, -d, -ied	
looking for words that I can list as exceptions in my Writer's notebook or on my tablet	
checking the ending -tion (never spelled shun)	
My comment on my editing skills: *I have improved my editing skills by...*	
Teacher's comment with feedback:	

Investigating Plurals

You could continue work on word structure by investigating plurals with your students. Plurals vary greatly and the exceptions are interesting. To review common plural structures, you could read the "One Potato, Two Potatoes" chant to students, and have them say it chorally, rereading lines in pairs, either verifying that they knew an idea already or if they did not, determining what they learned, and what further questions they have.

One Potato, Two Potatoes
If you want to change one
to two or more,
here are three good ways to explore.
Add *e* and *s*; change *box* to *boxes*.
Then go on to change *fox* to *foxes*.
Brushes follows that same rule,
but it does not work for *school*.
School has the most common ending:
Just add *s* to make it *schools*,
as *book* to *books*, and *rule* to *rules*.
Can you find change number 3?
Baby to *babies*, *berry* to *berries*,
candy to *candies*, *cherry* to *cherries*.
Take time to inquire. Take time to explore
how to change one into many more.

As this rhyme conveys, there are three common ways to make plurals: by adding *es*, by adding *s*, and by changing *y* to *i* and adding *es*.

After a group discussion relating to what students know about plurals, it may be helpful to have students work in pairs, and from a page of the text each student is reading, list the plurals they find and see if they fit into one of the three main categories. There may be exceptions, but you have created awareness and a spirit of investigation, which they can use as they edit their written work that day. You may find it interesting to note how common the use of plural form is in both their reading and writing then and for a few subsequent days.

It is inevitable that students will want to talk about the exceptions, so before they do this as a whole group, you may want to read the "One Potato, Two Potatoes" chant, give students time to talk about how it matches what they have observed, and then lead a lively discussion on the structure of plurals and their interesting exceptions. When students are given ownership of their learning like this, I have found, their engagement is quite remarkable. Their observations may surprise and delight you.

Discovering irregular plurals

When challenged to think about words, students impress me by the clarity of their observations. Consider this sentence that a Grade 3 student wrote:

> She is wise because she knows how to treat people and she knows how it is to have freinds.

What is surprising about this sample is that the student correctly spelled the irregular plural *people* and added *-s* to "freind," but reversed the *ie* in that same word. However, *friend* is third on the list of commonly misspelled words in Grade 3, so perhaps the error is not so surprising, after all!

Students might be interested to know that the Germanic form of plurals (e.g., *house, housen; shoe, shoen*) was eventually displaced by the French method of making plurals, namely, adding an *s* (e.g., *house, houses; shoe, shoes*). Only a few words have retained their Germanic plurals, *men, oxen, feet, teeth*, and *children* among them.

This information may help students to remember these few exceptions and find a few others such as these:

mouse, mice; louse, lice; tooth, teeth; foot, feet; goose, geese

Language Living and Changing

Mongoose is an uncommon word, in that it comes to English from Hindi, and because its plural is not *mongeese* as might be expected, but *mongooses*. However, *mongeese* is becoming widely accepted — and language is living and changes. Note that *mongooses* matches *nooses* and *cabooses*.

Plural words that break the change-*y*-to-*i*-rule have a rule of their own. If a word ends in a consonant plus *y* as in *baby*, the *y* is changed to *i* and *es* is added; however, if the word ends in a vowel plus *y*, as in *key*, only *s* is added. Not so many words do this, but here are a few:

jay, jays; monkey, monkeys; donkey, donkeys;
turkey, turkeys; journey, journeys; toy, toys

Words ending in *o* tend to add *es* to make the plural word, for example,

tomato, tomatoes; potato, potatoes; hero, heroes;
domino, dominoes; volcano, volcanoes; mango, mangoes

But there are not many of these words.

In relatively few cases, just adding *s* creates the plural word, as in

radio, radios; piano, pianos, video, videos; taco, tacos;
zoo, zoos; burrito, burritos; soprano, sopranos

Words ending in *x*, *ch*, *sh*, and *ss* add *-es*. Typical examples include

box, boxes; fox, foxes; church, churches; ditch, ditches;
dish, dishes; brush, brushes; class, classes; dress, dresses

Students can try to find more words for this pattern, but basically, telling them that they can hear the *-es* when they say the word should enable them to spell it. They should not find this pattern a problem.

There are also some plurals in transition. The traditional rule is to change *f* to *v* and add *-es* as in

scarf, scarves; calf, calves; half, halves; self, selves; elf, elves;
life, lives; wife, wives; knife, knives; wolf, wolves; loaf, loaves

However, it seems Disney started the trend to *-fs* with *Snow White and the Seven Dwarfs*, so we tend to see *hoof, hoofs*, and *roof, roofs*. It may be just a matter of time before other words follow!

Moving towards self-monitoring of editorial skills

Again, this information on plurals is of little use to students unless it can be applied to their writing. You may have decided to build student word knowledge on plurals because it is on your list of common student errors, or you may have observed a number of students having problems with plurals. Addressing student need would be appropriate and totally relevant to their work. For certain, at some time, students will have problems with some plurals as they write, so this topic does need to be addressed.

After working with plurals, an editing checklist could look like this, or you could customize it to what students are currently learning about words:

I can edit by . . .	
checking plurals with *es*, *s*, or changing *y* to *i* and adding *es*	
checking for plurals that are exceptions and keeping an ongoing list (e.g., *child*, *children*)	

Students can find editing written work daunting; therefore, it is worthwhile for them to edit only after revision has taken place, and they are getting ready to publish their work. To be successful, students would look for only one or two items at a time.

Peer editors can help — you will have students at expert level in various categories. Encourage all students to be expert in one category, for example, in a wider range of editing tasks, checking for words with double letters, or checking for words lacking double letters that should have them. Students can display cards that note their editing expertise on their desks or wear tags that identify their areas of expertise.

Poetry and reading responses are sometimes easier to edit, as they are often shorter than other written forms such as a report or a persuasive text.

EXPERT EDITOR
Specialty: checking for the ending *-tion*

EXPERT EDITOR
Specialty: checking for plurals

As student editors hone their skills, they will be able to give positive verbal descriptive feedback, for example, saying, "I have noticed that you are so much better at finding words that have plural endings. You made it easy for me to edit."

One skill that students in Grades 4 through 6 and beyond acquire is the ability to write longer pieces, so it is important in the craft of writing that these pieces of writing have something to say: that the goal is not the length of the piece, but the quality of the writing.

The goal of editing for students is that they will eventually be able to self-monitor. As they go through Grades 4, 5, and 6, it is important that they identify through self-assessment and ongoing descriptive feedback from the teacher and others which editing skills they can use to self-monitor and which skills they are working on. Students might keep an ongoing checklist as demonstrated below.

List of Editing Skills	I think I need more practice, with comment	I think I can self-monitor as I edit
Plurals		• I can check for most plurals.
Double consonants	I am still learning more about doubling consonants.	• I know all the common words that double consonants when you add *-ing*.

Students need to consistently share what they are learning about words as they edit because doing so helps build class knowledge, they become expert in certain areas, and in addition to asking questions of the teacher, they can ask one another relevant questions.

Compound Words: Wordplay with a Difference

Because English is a living, growing language, many words change over time, and constantly changing among these are words that have been compounded or put together over time. As they change from two words into one, sometimes they are hyphenated for awhile, and then they are joined.

Let it snow!

Living in a country known for its snowy winters, students tend to know a large number of words containing the word *snow*. Because one of the structural searches for words is compound words, a challenge would be to ask students to find 12 or more compound words containing *snow*. The results might surprise them! Here are 22 they might find:

snowball	snowman	snowbank	snowmobile
snowbelt	snowplough	snowbird	snowscape
snowblower	snowblower	snowboard	snowshoe
snowbrush	snowstorm	snowdrift	snowsuit
snowdrop	snowmaking	snowfall	snowmen
snowflake	snowfort		

Snow angel is still two words, but they may think it one. If students learn to spell *snow*, they will be able to accurately spell the beginnings of 22 words, as well as derivatives from *snow*, such as *snowy, snowing, snowed, snows*.

Then, if they are focused on snow, you could encourage them to consider descriptive words that will help to enrich their writing: *blizzard, frost, frosty, icy, sleet, snow flurry, snow blanket, snow shower*, and so on.

Riddling with Compound Words

Creating riddles or questions related to words on their list is an activity I have found to be instructive and enjoyable for students. They can find graphic images from the computer and ask questions about them, as I have done. For example, I have shown an image of a white flower and asked, "Is this a cowslip or a snow-drop?" A simpler question would be to provide the image of a snowshoe and ask, "Is this a snowshoe or a snowboard?" A more complex question related to a study of medieval times might be to show the image of a crossbow and ask, "Is this a crossbar or a crossbow?"

Although we are playing with words and creating compound words, we must never forget that what matters most in words is their meaning, and the writer's interest in using them to convey meaning.

Building compound word lists

Students enjoy generating lists of compound words that are built from certain beginnings, such as *air, back, butter, cow*, and *cross*. The next page lists some of the words they can build.

air	back	butter	cow	cross
airbrush	backstroke	buttercup	cowbird	crossbar
airport	backfield	butterfingers	cowboy	crossbeam
airplane	backfire	butterfly	cowhide	crossbones
airline	background	buttermilk	cowslip	crossbow
	backhand			crosscurrent
	backlog			crossroad
	backstop			crosswalk
	backtrack			
	backwater			
	backwoods			

For further work on compounds, I will suggest a few more words from which students can create lists: *day, ear, foot, house,* and *news.* Here are some possibilities.

day	ear	foot	house	news
daybreak	earache	football	houseboat	newscast
daydream	eardrum	footbridge	housecoat	newsletter
daylight	earmark	footstep	housefly	newspaper
daytime	earmuff	foothill	housekeeper	newsprint
	earphone	footstool	housewife	newsreel
	earring	footlights	housework	
	earwig	footlocker		
		footman		
		footnote		
		footpath		
		footprint		
		footrest		

You may find that students want to come back to this activity as they discover compound words in their reading and writing that cause them to want to create more words. Searching for words is an activity that seems to provide energy all on its own, and engagement with words is how students will grow as writers. One gift you can give students is to encourage them to add words to their ever-increasing vocabulary, and to use them as they write.

Searching for land: A personal stake

While working with compound words in this way, a Grade 5 student once said, "I wonder if there are lots of compound words for *land*. I know four." And so the search began. The class first came up with words ending in *land* and then developed a list of words beginning with *land*. This is the list they generated after a number of days:

> mainland, grassland, headland, homeland
> farmland, marshland, highland, lowland, inland
> parkland, swampland, wasteland
> landfall, landholder, landlocked, landlord
> landmark, landslide, landfill, landlady
> landline, landmass, landlubber, landowner

The students did well partly because of their access to lists on the computer but also because of a link with geographical terms the class had been using. Their ongoing enthusiasm for the activity grew out of one wondering student's interest, something that became infectious as other joined in. Encourage your students to wonder about and search for words, too!

Students become seriously involved when they generate the inquiry because they have a personal stake in it. They can also involve their friends or a partner in a word-related inquiry and share the knowledge they gain, which renews self-motivation and engagement. As always, the goal is to have our students feeling involved, engaged, and growing as word users and writers.

4

Many Words, Many Questions

If you encourage students to ask questions about words, you will be pleasantly surprised by some of their questions and wonder statements. You will also gain an opportunity to respond with some practical information or to set students the task of investigating to find out more about their wonderings. The goal is always to have a community of learners, asking questions and engaged in inquiry.

Not long ago, Grade 5 students were prompted to raise some questions about words. Here are some of the questions they asked:

"Who invented English?" is a great student investigation, and ongoing research can be shared.

"Who invented English?"
"Why are there silent letters because what's the point about them in words if they're silent?"
"Why do we need dictionaries?"
"Why do we need to use vowels?"
"Are there more *oi* words or *oy* words?"
"Why is there a *u* after every *q*?"
"If *ph* would be replaced by *f*, would it make language any easier?"
"Why are the words in Canada different from the words in America?"

And here are some of their wonderings:

"I wonder why we have compound words like *tomboy* and *cowboy*."
"I wonder why *y* is sometimes a vowel.
"I wonder if the words in Canada are different than the words in America."
"I wonder why do two letters make one sound."

Any of the questions above can be treated as an investigation. For example, you and your students can explore answers to "Why are there silent letters, because what's the point about them in words if they're silent?" This question can be dealt with at the same time as "Why do we need dictionaries?"

"Why are there silent letters . . .?"

Silent letters at the beginning of words make those words the most difficult to access in dictionaries, so we as teachers need to help students build knowledge about them. The easiest way to deal with silent letters is to surprise students by introducing words where the silent letter has a sound in some forms of the word and then introducing the word where the same letter is silent. If students make the link, they will remember how to spell that word. Using a chant may help.

The Sounds of Silence
Did you know
that silent letters
sometimes have a sound?
In *signal* you hear *g*;
In *sign* you don't.
In *bombard* you hear *b*;
In *bomb*, you won't.
In *crumble*, you hear *b*;
In *crumb*, you don't.
In *twins* you hear *w*;
In *two* you won't.
The fact that silent letters can be heard —
Does this not strike you as absurd?

I would prompt students to refer to the chant and match words where the letters make sound (e.g., *bombard*) with base words with silent letters, *bomb*, *crumb*, and *two* among them. They could create a T-chart, with words where the letters make sound on the left and words that have the silent letter on the right.

Ask students whether they notice that three of the following six italicized words have something in common — *autumnal, autumn; solemnity, solemn; columnist, column*. *mn* is the combination where *m* and *n* are heard at first, then *n* is silent. You might also note that *g* and *n* are heard in *signature* and *resignation* but are silent in *sign* and *resign*.

Investigation: Silent letters and the /n/ sound

It is important for students to know that silent letters do not have infinite possibilities. If a word begins with the sound /n/ but not the letter *n*, then there are only three alternatives: *gn*, *kn*, and *pn*. Since *pn* is largely related to medical terms such as *pneumonia* and *pneumococcal*, the silent *p* will rarely be used in student writing. However, students could be encouraged to complete an inquiry as to which combination occurs most often at the beginning of words: *kn* or *gn*. When I have asked teachers to do this during workshops I was conducting, they enjoyed it.

Students enjoy the exercise, too. I have had them take up the challenge and stick with it over a number of days. When I tell them, after they have struggled to find words for their *gn* list, that they can probably find six words beginning with *gn*, they feel relieved. (There are six more, but, I think, it may be difficult for them to find the other six.) It is important that students predict which one will have most words on the list — *gn* or *kn*. It is often an evenly split prediction because they encounter the word *gnome* in Grade 1 and think this is a fairly common beginning.

There are, however, only a few *gn* words, the more common being *gnome*, *gnat*, *gnu*, *gnarl*, *gnash*, and *gnaw*. The six more uncommon *gn* words are *gneiss*, *gnomon* (marker on a sundial), *gnostic*, *gnocci*, *gnotobiotic*, *gnosis*; then, most other words are extensions of these (e.g., *gnarl*, *gnarly*, *gnarled*, *gnarls*).
Many words begin with *kn*. There are at least 200, including these:

knack, knap, knapsack, knead, knee, kneecap, knead, kneel
knell, knife, kneepad, knew, knickers, knight, knit, knob

knock, knockwurst, knoll, knot, know, knowledge, knuckle

mn has only two words — *mnemonic* and *mnemonics* — so it is not really a contender. *kn* is the most likely alternative.

Students will find additional words as extensions of some of these. For example, *know* can become *knowledge, knowledgeable, knows, knowing, knowingly,* and *known.* Since some students will challenge these words as "cheating," it is important to establish up front that adding to base words is all right. Students do not need to find every word that begins with *kn,* so much as they need to recognize it as a more likely beginning than *gn.*

This investigation should help students to remember that when they look up a word in a dictionary with the sound /n/ at the beginning, but not the letter *n,* they should first try *kn,* then *gn,* and then *pn.*

Computer spellcheckers need a certain number of correct letters before they can be of help. They may even suggest quite odd alternative words.

Silent letters to look out for

Here is a list of letters that may give students trouble because they are not heard. Students could add the words with silent letters to their Writer's notebooks, lexical dictionaries, iPads, or tablets, as they need to use them. They could also add other words with silent letters that they use in their written work and that they may need to memorize. I have listed the silent letter at the beginning:

You may want to begin with the first few letters of the alphabet, and have students contribute the other words as they come across them in their work.

    b   crumb, debt, doubt, lamb, plumber, subtle
    c   acquaint, indict
    d   handsome, handkerchief
    g   sign, gnaw
    h   heir, khaki, exhibit, ghost
    k   knee, know
    l   calm, talk, walk, would
    n   autumn, condemn
    p   pneumonia, cupboard, psalm
    s   island, debris
    t   tsunami, listen, castle, whistle, mortgage
    w   write, answer

Note that these are all single silent letters. As far I as I know, *th* in *asthma,* and *ch* in *fuchsia* are the only two silent pairs, but they need to be noted as they give writers a headache.

Chanting with silent letters

One way to engage students in working with silent letters is to have them create chants. Two samples appear at the top of the next page. The chant on the left is a two-part chant to reinforce silent letters (part 1 for the teacher, part 2 for the students). The students can repeat it, as desired. The chant on the right can be adapted for other letters by the students themselves, or in collaboration with the teacher, and repeated as desired:

Cheer for G & B	Cheer for W
1: Sound off.	1: Sound off.
2: *G, B.*	2: *W.*
1: Sound off.	1: Sound off.
2: Fine by me!	2: Here's your cue.
1: Give me a silent *G*.	1: Give me a silent *W*.
2: Sign.	2: Two.
1: Need to hear it!	1: Need to hear it!
2: Signal.	2: Twice!
1: Give me a silent *B*.	1: Can't hear you!
2: Crumb.	2: Twenty.
1: Can't hear it!	1: Another one?
2: Crumble.	2: Twins.
1: What do we know?	1: What do we know?
2: They can be quiet.	2: They can be quiet.
1: What do we know?	1: What do we know?
2: They can be heard.	2: They can be heard.

There is much information here on silent letters in response to one student's question. You would not share it all at once, but do so over time, so that students can practise and consolidate their learning, and integrate this work with dictionary usage. Nonetheless, by taking the time to explore a student's question, you validate it, show respect, and convey the idea that pursuing the answer is worthwhile.

Trying to "Show Off" with Silent Letters

Students may find it interesting to know that a number of silent letters were added to the language as a way to "improve" the English words and link them to their Latin roots. During the Renaissance, great prestige was given to the languages of ancient Greece and Rome. English scholars decided to change the spelling of some words to match Latin roots. Consequently, they added a *b* to *debt* to link it to Latin *debitum* and they added a *p* to *receipt* to link it to Latin *recipere*, which means to receive. But ordinary people continued to pronounce the words the same way, so the letters stayed silent.

Until about 25 years ago, Latin was taught in many high schools, and so the link was reinforced. Now students can still "show off" to their parents by sharing this information.

"Why do we need dictionaries?"

Often, students think of dictionaries as references for words they don't know how to spell, where they can access a word only if they already have a reasonable idea of how to spell it. Anyone looking at dictionaries in this way would not consider them helpful.

Dictionaries, however, can be extremely helpful to students. As you will know, they have two main functions: first, to allow someone to check the spelling of a word; and second, to enable someone to find the meaning or multiple meanings of a word.

On top of their basic functions, dictionaries are a fund of information.

- Each page has separate entries, and each word being defined has bold print.
- The word in bold print is usually followed by characters that explain how to pronounce the word.
- The part of speech is then given (e.g., noun).
- Then the meaning or several meanings, if appropriate, are given.
- Many dictionaries also provide word origins.

Sometimes, so much information can seem overwhelming, which is why students need much practice in using dictionaries. In order to look up a word in a dictionary, they need a knowledge of alphabetical order and at least the first few letters of the word. They will benefit from having the following understandings.

- Students need to realize that they do not start at the beginning of the dictionary text and leaf their way through the book, to check the spelling of a word beginning with *s*, for example. They need practice in finding certain letters in the dictionary quickly. They could begin by locating the pages where their first and last names would appear, using these as a base for other searches.
- Students need to learn to use the guide words, which are typically at the top of the page. First guide word is the first word to be defined on the page; last guide word is the last word to be defined on the page.
- Finally, students need to appreciate the fund of information they can find in just a single word entry.

Some dictionaries are called "spelling dictionaries," and sometimes students will find it faster to use one of these to locate a word they are unable to spell. A variety of dictionaries is a vital part of the literacy program, as some contain more information and word connotations than others. Beyond checking for spelling, you will want to capture in students a love for words, so that they become interested in reading about words in a dictionary.

There are free and for-sale apps related to "Merriam-Webster Dictionary." There is also a Word of the Day feature, which can be sent to an email address.

Dictionary usage has been revolutionized by online dictionaries and wide student use of laptops and tablets. Students will find it much easier and faster to find a word electronically once they know how to "google" it or use another search engine to find it. An excellent online source for this would be Merriam-Webster at www.merriam-webster.com. Not only does this site have a dictionary, which reads the word aloud and provides detailed meaning, including word origins, but it also contains a thesaurus.

Beyond that, nearly every laptop or tablet has a built-in spellchecker, but this tool has limitations. Spellcheckers do not catch every word that is wrong. If someone types "form" but means "from," the spellchecker will not catch the error; there would either have to be a complex built-in grammar checker or a proofreader reading for sense. Spellcheckers can introduce errors, too. One of my younger students once wrote, "I like ice cream alot." The spellchecker changed it to "I like ice cream allot." When I pointed out to him that he had missed a letterspace rather than spelling the word wrongly, he grinned and said, "I told my mom I spelled it correctly, but she said the computer had to be correct!" We must encourage our students to always think about words and never simply accept the adjustment of a spellchecker.

Because students text so much nowadays, they may have some stories of a text that was changed by the spellchecker to another word, which changed the meaning of what they wrote. Some of these stories will be funny, some cautionary. For example, I wrote to a friend to say, "I would like to see you when you have some time," and for some reason the spellchecker changed it to "I would like to see you when you have done time." I am so glad I caught this!

What students can do when they want to spell a word but can't find it

To prevent students from being lost in a sea of words in the dictionary, it is important for them to know that *most* of the time consonants stay true to sound, so, if they hear a *b* at the beginning of a word, the word will likely begin with *b*. Unless students understand that the number of alternatives is limited, they will become discouraged and feel that there is no logic to English spelling. There are, however, many patterns to prove that there is logic. Here is a list of possible alternatives that students can discover through investigation, as shown earlier in this chapter, or through simply noting them when they come across them and talking about them with others.

Consonants:
1. If you look up a word that sounds as if it begins with *f* but it doesn't, try *ph* (e.g., *photo*).
2. If you look up a word with the sound of *g* plus a vowel, but it isn't there, try *gh* (e.g., *ghost*).
3. If you look up a word that sounds as if it begins with *n* but it doesn't, try *kn*, then *gn*, then *pn* (*mn* would be very uncommon).
4. If you look up a word that sounds as if it begins with *k* (e.g., *kept, kabob, kangaroo*), but it doesn't, try *c* (e.g., *cab, cake, cat*) or *ch* (e.g., *chaos, chemistry, chasm, chameleon, character, chord* — not so common).
5. If you look up a word that sounds as if it begins with *kw*, usually you would try *qu* (e.g., *quack, quick*). Exceptions: *Kwanza, kwacha* (currency in Zambia and Malawi)
6. If you look up a word that sounds as if it begins with *j* but it doesn't, try *g* (e.g., *gem, geography, gerbil, geometry, gesture, giant, giraffe*).
7. If you look up a word that sounds as if it begins with *r* but it doesn't, try *wr* (e.g., *wrist*).
8. If you look up a word that sounds as if it begins with *s* but it doesn't, try *c* (e.g., *city*), then *sc* (e.g., *scene*), then *ps* (e.g., *psychology, psycho, psychiatrist*).
9. If you look up a word that sounds as if it begins with *t* plus a vowel but it doesn't, try *thy* (*thyme*), then *pt* — but this is very rare (e.g, *pterodactyl, ptarmigan*).
10. If you look up a word that sounds as if it begins with *o* but it doesn't, try *h* (e.g., *honest, hour*).
11. If you look up a word that sounds as if it begins with *w* plus a vowel but it doesn't, try *wh* (e.g., *when, why, where*).
12. If you look up a word that sounds as if it begins with *z* but doesn't, try *x* (e.g., *xylophone, xylem, xylene, xylophagus* — very uncommon).

Unpredictable Vowels

Vowels can be very unpredictable. My favorite example of this was when a Grade 1 student told me that *elephant* began with *l*, and I said, "Listen to me — ehh . . . lephant." He then said, "That's not how I say it. Listen — lllll . . . ephant." Later, I drew a sketch of an elephant with an *e* on each ear and an *l* on its trunk to help him to spell the beginning of the word. However, I am convinced that he spelled it that way to please me, not because he believed it was correct!

Vowels:

If a word sounds as if it starts with a vowel, but it doesn't, try the other vowels, until you find it. Investigations into such matters are important because they will help students realize that they should not rely too heavily on sound.

When students have completed some investigations with silent letters, and you have finished reinforcing some of this knowledge through discussion, by teaching a mini-lesson, or by teaching a whole-group lesson, it is often useful to have students apply their findings directly to their writing. The editing checklist for that day might look like this:

I can edit by . . .	Student Comment	Teacher Comment
checking for silent letters in words — I have chosen two examples from the list to check.	I will pay attention to silent letters in my writing, and editing.	
When I look up a word that sounds as if it begins with *n* but it isn't *n*, I will try *kn*, *gn*, *pn*, and make a note of these words.	know, knocked, knob	
When I spell a word that sounds as if it begins with *kw* but it doesn't, usually I will try *qu*.	quest, quickly	

This editing checklist can be customized by the students according to their needs. The major point is that they *need to apply* their growing word knowledge directly to their editing.

How can I address students who are having trouble with . . .?"

As well as students wondering about words and asking questions about them, you probably notice common spelling problems as you read over student work, as you meet with students in writer's workshop, or as you talk with them individually about their writing. Here are some common issues on which to base your own "How can I address students who are having trouble with . . ." questions and solutions:

> contractions
> homonyms in their written work
> vowel pairs in their written work
> long vowels in their written work ("mak"/*make*)
> vowels with *r* (e.g., *far, fir, fur*)
> the editing process
> getting started in their writing

Just a few sample issues are addressed here, since it is probable that you already have many solutions. Please note that I am interested in taking part in an ongoing digital dialogue with you on many of these and other spelling questions. I invite you to get in touch with me through email. My email address is provided at the end of Chapter 8.

"How can I address students who are having trouble with . . . contractions?"

Students tend to confuse apostrophes in contractions with apostrophes showing possession. The word *it's* (meaning "it is") poses a particular problem. It is vital for students to learn that contractions have missing letters because this knowledge will help them to put the apostrophe in the right place. It is easy to teach and review this, but much harder for students to apply consistently. Apostrophes in possession are an ongoing struggle for students, not so much when the form is singular, as in *Mary's coat*, but when the form is plural, as in *the babies' toys*. For students, I think, we should keep the focus to learning about singular possession and contractions, and coach when needed with plural possession.

Missing Letters in Contractions

Verb *to be*
I am — I'm
You are — you're
He is — he's
She is — she's
It is — it's
We are — we're
They are — they're

Verb *to have*
I have — I've
You have — you've
We have — we've
They have — they've

Words with *not*
is not — isn't
cannot — can't
could not — couldn't
do not — don't
did not — didn't
does not — doesn't
has not — hasn't
have not — haven't
should not — shouldn't
was not — wasn't
will not — won't
would not — wouldn't

Future tense
I will — I'll
You will — You'll
We will — We'll
They will — They'll

Miscellaneous
Let us — Let's
of the clock — o'clock

Perhaps the most common misspelling of all the contractions is *you're*, so that is one to highlight and come back to often. I notice that the spellchecker will put in the apostrophe, even when you text, and if you change *you're* to "ur" on a cellphone, it may change it to "u'r."

"How can I address students who are having trouble with . . . homonyms in their written work?"

Here is another issue commonly raised by teachers in response to student work samples. In any event, you may want students to explore homonyms as homo-

Students may want to write a verse something like this to remind them of how contractions work or just to have fun writing a short chant:

> If you want satisfaction,
> When you write a contraction,
> Make an apostrophe for letters
> That are missing in action.

graphs and homophones. Doing this may help them to remember some strategies to deal with these words. If, however, use of the terms *homographs* and *homophones* confuses the students in any way, just refer to them as "homonyms."

Homophones make perfect sense. The information that there is a good reason for words with the same sound to be spelled differently in English needs to be shared with students. Use of homophones significantly helps the reader. For example, "I lost a *pair* of gloves" instantly tells the reader that the person lost two gloves; if the sentence said, "The *pear* tasted delicious," the reader would know the word was referring to a piece of fruit. "I had to *pare* an apple for my friend" refers to the third spelling, where someone removed the skin from a piece of fruit. Each time, the spelling helps with meaning. If you changed them all to the same new spelling, maybe "*payr*," you would have to work out what was happening only by inference, a real challenge if the sentences were more complex. Basically, then, homophones are intended to help the reader get to meaning more quickly.

This chant may serve to introduce students to homophones or to revise their understanding of the term. Finding the homophones in the poem is not a difficult task. What is important is to know what each of the words means and which meaning is associated with which spelling.

Meaning Makers
Did you know that
homophones have purpose?
They bring different meanings to words.
So *pear* and *pair* and *pare*
mean something different.
So do *hare* and *hair*,
herd and *heard*.

Since meaning is important, I recommend that you and your class build lists like the one below, with students providing the meanings.

Word	Explanation	Homophone for That Word	Explanation
aisle	passageway	isle	island
bare	naked	bear	animal; to carry
beach	sand/rocks at edge of lake or ocean	beech	tree
blew	past tense of *blow*	blue	color
brake	something you apply to stop	break	to drop and have object fall apart; to have a short time off, as coffee break
cereal	grain-based breakfast food	serial	a TV program with installments
die	to stop living	dye	to change color

Word	Explanation	Homophone for That Word	Explanation
fair	reasonable and just; a place with rides and food (e.g., fall fair)	fare	cost of a journey
fir	tree	fur	thick hair on animal coat
flew	past tense of *fly*	flu (short form of *influenza*)	illness
flour	processed grain	flower	part of a plant
hair	covering on head	hare	animal

If you wish to see a longer list of homophones, check out the many lists on the Internet. Students need to learn meanings side by side to differentiate between them, but for spelling, it is important to list these words in patterns.

- *There* would be in the following pattern list related to place: *there, where, somewhere, anywhere, everywhere, nowhere.*
  Their would be listed with pronouns to help clarify link to usage: *my, your, his, her, our, their.* Most often, students do not misspell *there* and *their,* but they do tend to misuse them.
- Similarly, it is important to teach *to, too,* and *two* in separate pattern lists. *To* would be listed with short prepositions that have high frequency in writing: *to, as, at, but, for, in, of, on, up.* Of the three choices, *to* is used 98 percent of the time in writing — here's an example of when teaching homonyms is not helpful. *Two* should be taught two ways, first with its meaning links — *two, twice, twins, twenty* — and then with its number links — *one, two, three, four, five.* The third *too* should just be edited when necessary. Telling students that *too* is an adverb of degree is rarely helpful, but you could share a list of adverbs with *too* at the top. This list may be interesting to older students, but, I believe, what will help them most is to know that they use the word *to* 98 percent of the time.

  A more useful exercise would be to help students begin to list possible alternatives for *very,* perhaps *considerably, greatly, highly, really, vastly.* Seeing *too* and *very* in this context may help. A challenging question to ask would be this: What is the difference in meaning between these two sentences?

  She finished her homework very quickly. [more factual]
  She finished her homework too quickly. [more critical]

Since homophones are intended to convey meaning, students need to see them together in context in separate sentences to attach the correct meaning to the correct word. For spelling, though, the words need to be listed in a pattern context, such as **hair** with *chair, fair,* and *pair*; and **hare** with *bare, care, dare, glare, rare, pare, spare,* and *stare.*

Homographs are words that are spelled the same way, but differ in meaning. For example, consider: You *park* a car; you walk in a *park. Park* is a homograph. The following poem explores the homograph *set.*

Although *too* is used in Grade 1 writing, the adverb is not used so much after that: students progress beyond simple sentences such as "Jack came too."

Adverbs of Degree

too	*too* much
just	*just* right
nearly	*nearly* there
quite	*quite* good
so	*so* tasty
very	*very* close

Variations on *Set*

It is unusual for a homograph to have so many meanings. In this case, there are at least 20 more (e.g., to set the pace, to set up shop, a tea set, a TV set, to set a trap, to set a clock, to set a broken bone, to set a special date, to set a good example, to set a price, to set a ship's course, to set eyes on, to be a part of the jet set, a set of golf clubs, to set a world record, to set off a firework, to set out on a journey, to set the dog on someone, to set apart, to wait for concrete to set).

Homographs — Setting Them Straight

You can set up a table,
Set down a book,
Or set your jaw
With a nasty look.
Set sail in a yacht
Set plans in motion,
Set fire to something —
Not a good notion!
You can buy a chess set,
Or set someone straight.
You can set words to music,
To make you feel great!

You may want to suggest that students work together to find the meanings for the following homographs: *bat, change, clear, content,* display, park, permit,* recess,* research, rose, minute,* sewer,* wave,* and wind.** For some of these words, indicated here by an asterisk, the pronunciation changes when the meaning changes. You could ask students to try to identify which pronunciation goes with which meaning.

Both homophones and homographs tend to be referred to as "homonyms," and that is perfectly valid. I have made the distinction as they are slightly different concepts to explore. The labels are important only in linguistics, so the students can refer to them all as "homonyms," noting there are two different kinds. Since spelling is a thinking activity, though, sometimes the distinction helps students to see the logic of homophones. Below is a summary in Venn diagram format.

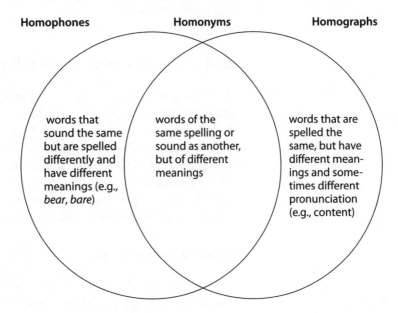

Homophones   **Homonyms**   **Homographs**

words that sound the same but are spelled differently and have different meanings (e.g., *bear, bare*)

words of the same spelling or sound as another, but of different meanings

words that are spelled the same, but have different meanings and sometimes different pronunciation (e.g., content)

As students build information about words and how they work, and come to a word they are unsure of, they can draw on their large "schema" of prior knowledge and make an informed prediction instead of a wild guess. In being able to do so, students will feel in control of their learning and know that they are building competency in spelling and editing. There is no need for them to be lost in a maze of words.

5

Towards Journey's End: Meaning Patterns

On the journey to becoming a knowledgeable word user and an informed word constructor, the learner needs to acquire knowledge of sound, function, and meaning patterns. In early grades *sound patterns* are a base for students to acquire phonological awareness and graphophonic knowledge related to consonant sounds, short and long vowel patterns, and silent letters. These are followed by *function patterns*, which involve the syntax of words, base words, inflectional endings, plurals, contractions, compound words, and endings for adjectives and adverbs. At the end of the journey are *meaning patterns*, which include wordplay (e.g., puns, riddles, and jokes), prefixes, suffixes, word origins, word narratives related to origins, idioms, and literary devices such as similes and metaphors. In this chapter the function patterns addressed include adding a suffix to a noun as a base word (e.g., *beauty, beautiful, beautifully*), adding a suffix to an adjective as a base word (e.g., *dim, dimly*), and adding *-er* or *-est* to adjectives. The meaning patterns include these: word origins, word narratives, idiomatic phrases, prefixes, and suffixes.

Building Knowledge of Meaning Patterns

To build a strong knowledge of meaning patterns, it would be relevant to have students explore how the English language has borrowed words from around the world. Most words used in English today find their origins elsewhere. English still derives many words from Latin and Greek, but it has also borrowed words from nearly all the languages in Europe and even further afield. From the period of the Renaissance up to the present, a steady stream of new words has flowed into the language. www.merriam-webster.com reports that more than 120 languages are on record as sources of present-day English vocabulary.

Relating to word origins

Students may be able to relate more to etymology, or the origins of words, if they begin with the origin of their last name. They may also want to poll their parents as to why their first name was chosen, and they can ask parents and family members about the meaning of their last name. An online site to aid with this is www.surnamedb.com, which outlines the history of hundreds of surnames, but mostly more common North American surnames. Another site that may also prove useful is surnames.behindthename.com/usage.php, which has a more global perspective and lists names under countries of origin.

He Who Must Not Be Named

Also of interest to some students would be www.mugglenet.com/books/name_origins_characters.shtml, which gives the origins of the names of characters in the Harry Potter books in alphabetical order.

Students may want to extend their exploration of surnames by comparing the number of countries represented in their class and the variety of surnames from these countries. This work may lead to an interest in word origins, as nothing is more personal than a person's name.

Exploring words from home countries

Many students have come to North America from other countries, or their parents or grandparents have immigrated here, so they may want to find out how many words have come into English from their home countries. Students could begin with a real or digital world map — many classrooms have a world map. They could then collect and post words, recording which countries contributed which words to the English language. They would probably need fold-down lists for France, Italy, and Greece, but the number of other countries of origin might surprise them. Recording word origins on a map would provide cross-integration with mapping skills.

This investigation could be initiated by just a few students but grow until all students take part. The information gleaned could be shared with other classes or presented at an assembly. The task could last for several months, allowing students to build a word wall of words and their origins.

Print Sources: For this activity a good print source to check out is *Penguin Wordmaster Dictionary*. Here are some of the words it outlines, as a way to get students started:

- Dutch—boom, deck, smuggle, dock, splice, buoy, skipper, yacht, cruise (p. 89)
- Hindi—bungalow, dinghy, khaki, shampoo, bangle (p. 88)
- Spanish—alligator, barricade, cigar, mosquito, veranda (p. 32)

Another recommended print source is the *Oxford Dictionary of Word Origins*, edited by Julia Cresswell, which tracks the evolution of words. For example, it tells the reader that *coffee* comes from the Arabic "qahwa" via Turkish "kahveh" and that *sugar* comes from Arabic "sukkar" (p. 21). *Arctic*, on the other hand, comes from the Greek "arktos," meaning "bear" (p. 22). It refers not to the polar bear, but to the Great Bear, or Ursa Major, a constellation in the north. A third example of how words evolve is *banana*. Originally from Africa, that word traveled to English through Portuguese and Spanish from Mande, a language group of West Africa (p. 36).

Nearly all dictionaries provide information on word origins, as well. One reliable source is the latest *Merriam-Webster Dictionary*, with more than 75 000 word definitions. You may have a variety of classroom print dictionaries to offer your students.

Web Sources: Encourage students to check the Internet for information on word origins. For example, under "English language" on Wikipedia, they can learn about how Old Norse words entered the English language, mainly from the Viking influence on England, between 800 and 1000 CE. Words from Old Norse include common words such as those that follow on page 72:

anger, awe, bag, big, birth, blunder, both, cake, call, cast, cosy, cross, cut, die, dirt, drag, drown, egg, flat, flounder, gain, get, gift, give, guess, guest, gust, hug, husband, ill, kid, law, leg, lift, likely, link, loan, loose, low, mistake, odd, race, raise, root, rotten, same, scale, scare, score, seat, seem, sister, skill, skin, skirt, skull, sky, stain, steak, sway, take, though, thrive, Thursday, tight, till (until), trust, ugly, want, weak, window, wing, wrong

Students may want to check out Wikipedia first, but because Wikipedia is open source knowledge, they should always confirm their discoveries through a second source, such as

- an online etymological dictionary at www.etymonline.com/ (developed by Douglas Harper, a historian, author, and journalist from Lancaster, Pennsylvania)
- www.merriam-webster.com/, which has word origins, a vocabulary quiz, a word of the day, and an app for iPads

Consider that, while the *Merriam-Webster* dictionary is a reliable source for word origins, a single source on the Internet could simply be "Joe's bright ideas." Just as all books are not equal, neither are all Internet sites, so emphasize to students that double sourcing is important, and that they will need to learn which online sources are the most reliable and credible.

Discovering and Creating Narratives About Words

Where Did These Words Come From?

The word *hippopotamus* comes from the Greek word *hippos*, meaning horse and *potamus*, meaning river. So, *hippopotamus* literally means *river horse*. Somehow, I don't think he would take well to being ridden! The description refers to his size and where he lives. This word came to England via the Romans, who used a hippodrome to have chariot race, involving horses. (page 331)

The word *rhinoceros* comes from the Greek word, *rhinokeros*, from *rhis* meaning nose and *keras*, horn. "Nose horn" describes the animal well, as his horn is a significant feature. The same Greek word for nose, *rhino*, is used in rhinology, the study of the nose, and rhinoplasty, surgery on the nose. (page 597)

These word narrative models both come from *Penguin Wordmaster Dictionary*.

The origins of words, especially words derived from someone's name (e.g., sandwich), may seem somewhat random to students, but once they look more deeply, they will usually find some order. Consider, for example, the origins for the words *hippopotamus* and *rhinoceros* (at left).

Knowing word origins can pique interest in word study and help students to remember spellings. Many words lend themselves to the development of a real or perceived back story.

Back stories

People remember narrative more easily than isolated words since we tend to link story with images; therefore, students could represent word narratives by making up stories like the examples below, which are embellished truth. The information about the hippopotamus is true — and it is important that the derivation is true — but otherwise poetic licence can be taken.

Example 1:

Many years ago, an English traveler sailed all the way to Rome. Shortly after he arrived, he went to a grand show at the Hippodrome. The show opened with a parade of animals, many of which he had never seen. His favourite animal was grey, with tiny ears and a wide smile. It had a huge body and short legs, that seemed almost unable to support its bulk, and the traveler thought it was out of its element on land. It seemed as if it should be in water. He had to know what it was called. He asked his Roman friend who said, "We call it Hippopotamus, which means river horse. There is no word in your language for it." "Hippopotamus, you say." The man smiled. "I can't wait to tell my friends."

The suggested pattern for ending each narrative could be

"[focus word], you say." The man smiled. "I can't wait to tell my friends."

Example 2:

A weary traveler arrived in London, England. He came from Greece, but had gone off to explore the world, including making several trips to Africa. He told his London friends how he had been hiking through the grassland, heading for the forest in East Africa, when he was startled by large creatures he had never seen before. These animals were grey, huge, and to his relief, were eating only plants and twigs. When he looked at their odd-looking horns, they seemed to have two enormous noses! He did not know the local name for this creature, but "Nose horn" seemed to describe the animal well. So he told his friends, "I called it 'rhinokeros,' which means nose horn. There is no word in your language for it either." "Rhinoceros, you say." His listeners smiled. "We can't wait to tell our friends."

Creating narratives like these can be an engaging way to involve students in telling stories about the origins of words. It may also help to create in them a lifelong interest in words.

As noted above, an excellent print source for word origins is *Oxford Dictionary of Word Origins* edited by Julia Cresswell (Oxford University Press, 2010). A few engaging and model word narratives from that source appear below.

ambulance First used in the Crimean War, an ambulance was originally a mobile temporary hospital — a field hospital — that followed an army from place to place. The term was later applied to a wagon or cart used for carrying wounded soldiers off the battlefield, which in turn led to its modern meaning. Ambulance comes from the French *hôpital ambulant*, literally "walking hospital." (p. 14)

bed The core idea of this Old English word may be "digging," as if the very first beds were dug-out lairs or hollows. Medieval uses of **to make a bed** refer to the preparation of a sleeping place on the floor of an open hall, one which would not have existed until "made." (p. 42)

chat In medieval times chat was formed as a shorter version of **chatter**, which itself started life as an imitation of the sound made by people chatting away, rather as **jabber** and **twitter** imititated the sound they described . . . The success of the website called **Twitter** has led to heated debate among users as to whether what they do should be called to twitter or to tweet — yet another word imitating the sound of birds. (p. 81)

Connecting Chocolate Bars to Word Origins

The Aero chocolate bar is intriguing because the name derives from the Greek *aer* through the French word *aero*, meaning "air." As the chocolate has lots of air bubbles, the name is most appropriate. The prefix *aero-* used to be more common, but it remains in more complex words such as those at top left of the next page:

---

aerobics	From Greek *aer* meaning "air" and *bios*, "live," so a person who does aerobics "lives in air."
aerospace	This word could create some interesting cross-curricular discussion, since there is no air in space.
aerosol	Although this substance comes from a pressurized container, the origin of the word is *aero-* plus the first part of English **sol**ution.
aeronautics	The word for the study of the history of flight comes from the Greek *naus*, or ship; this is the study of "ships in the air."
aerial	The suffix *-al* is used to make adjectives, so this means "being in air."

More often, we use *air*, which makes life easier, as in *airbag, airborne, airbus, aircraft, airfare, airfreight, airline, airmail, airplane, airsickness, airstrip,* and *airwaves*. The word *airplane* is especially interesting in that the second part of the word, *plane*, comes from the Greek word *planos*. An airplane is literally an air wanderer. If you shorten this word to *plane* and are "catching a plane," are you catching a wanderer? Perhaps this idea would be of interest in writing poetry . . .

Photo essays, videos, and bluffing

Students can present word origins as photo essays, which they comment on and present to their peers, or as podcasts that they share. They may even create a video, illustrating idioms.

Just as the game Balderdash uses obscure English words and involves players in bluffing others with false meanings, students could challenge one another by giving a word origin narrative that is true and one that they have made up, then have other students guess which one is correct. They may even be able to create an online game, and challenge others in the online community. Alternatively, they could create a board game around this theme.

Exploring words from a range of language sources

For further investigation, the teacher may want to suggest that students look for words from any of the three main language contributors to English: the Germanic languages (which include Old Norse, Old/Middle English, and Dutch), French, and Latin. About 29 percent of words adopted from other languages came from French. Among the hundreds of words are *ambulance, diplomat, parachute,* and *sauce*. Some students may want to create a list of these to share. About another 29 percent of English words came from Latin: these include *agenda, circus,* and *data*. The Germanic languages contributed about 26 percent of adopted words into English, including *dollar, muffin,* and *Kindergarten* (which describes young children as being in a "children's garden"). About 6 percent of English words come from the Greek. These include such common words as *athlete, democracy,* and *museum*. Students can add to this list.

Students will be particularly interested in words from the language or languages they know other than English. In our multi-ethnic, multilingual culture, this connection has never been more important than it is today. Many of our students are bilingual and even trilingual. I remember clearly one student becoming excited because he was able to link French *soleil* with *solar* in English. Words can excite and challenge students every day, and we want to create a learning community in the classroom where this is the norm.

An excellent website, where countries or languages are listed in alphabetical order, is www.krysstal.com/borrow.html. Encourage students to explore this site or one like it and find their own words. In addition to information on the three main language sources, they will discover details such as these:

Cree — opossum, skunk
Czech — polka, robot
Egyptian — ebony, ivory, paper
Hindi — jungle, basmati, samosa, sari

Hungarian — coach, goulash, paprika, sabre
Inuit — husky, igloo, kayak
Italian — opera, umbrella, alarm, broccoli, macaroni
Japanese — judo, karate, tycoon

You could also have students generate another shorter list of words related to country names: these include African violet, Canadian bacon, Dutch barn, Irish stew, Spanish onion, and Welsh rarebit.

It is important for students to see language as growing, living, and changing all the time. New words are added every day to describe things we have no words for in English. Recent examples are *buzzword, carjacking, chatroom, cloud computing, couch potato, emoticon, flash mob, flash drive,* and *netbook*. You could suggest that students keep lists of recently added words. For example, if they check the Merriam-Webster online dictionary (www.merriam-webster.com/info/new_words.htm), they could find words added in 2006, for example, *mouse potato, spyware,* and *drama queen.* They could also check out which words were new in 1806!

Two ways to engage students in researching word origins

A group of students could create a short chant and present it to the class, showing words they discovered and their country of origin. The purpose would be to share information, remember less usual spellings, and have fun with words. Here is a sample chant:

Words from other countries
can be difficult to spell.
Italian gave us *macaroni*
and *broccoli*, as well.

Another way to engage students in researching word origins and thereby exploring how words are spelled is to put two words from the same country together and have a little fun with them. For example, using *robot* and *polka*, which are both Czech, a small group of students can devise a kind of dance called the "robot polka." They can then demonstrate this as other students repeat a simple chant:

Words cannot describe this.
What do I see?
Can someone please explain it to me?
What is it? Could it be . . .
The robot polka?

If the moves are simple, they could be taught to the class, and one student could hold up a piece of card with "robot polka" written on it to emphasize the words. Students may want to try other pairs of words from certain countries to create chants or short skits, as well. They could imagine a judo tycoon, a broccoli opera, a samosa jungle, or a husky kayak. This kind of exploration provides a jumping-off point and a reason to investigate a site such as www.krysstal.com/borrow.html for new words, which, in turn, could lead to some very creative writing.

How Adopting Words into English Has Affected the Spelling of English Words

Over the centuries, English has borrowed words from other languages that people have been exposed to through trading or being conquered. As indicated earlier, words were assimilated into English from Old Norse, Germanic languages, Latin, Danish, French, Greek, Arabic, Spanish, Italian, and Dutch. So, for example, a Dutch word such as *jacht* was adopted into English as *yacht* because there was no equivalent in English spelling. The addition of such words greatly enriched the English language but tended to create spelling exceptions. Here are some other examples.

1. Plural words have been influenced by German.

Some of our exceptions in plurals may have come from German plurals. For example, it is thought that the German plural form influenced the English plurals *oxen*, *children*, *brethren*, and *women*. The German plural of *pfau* (peacock) is *pfauen* and the plural of *Frau* (woman) is *Frauen*. So, *en* is used in the plural form, but in modern English we rarely use *en* now to create plurals.

2. The -*le* ending was adopted from French.

When William the Conqueror became king of England, Norman French became the language of the court and the educated people, whereas English was spoken by the common people. As a result, over time many French words were adopted into English, and some English words were changed because it was considered more educated to end words with -*le*. As a result, for example, the Middle English word *littel* became *little*.

Today, more than 3000 words in English end in -*le* and barely 400 end in -*el*, so about 75 percent of the time, it is correct to write -*le* at the end of the word. In student writing the percentage of -*le* words may be higher, as many -*el* words are not in common usage. The list below could be generated by students and added to over time—exceptions are the words to be committed to memory.

Words ending in -*le*		Words ending in -*el*
able	cycle	cancel
agreeable	female	easel
angle	gentle	funnel
article	juggle	hazel
battle	little	jewel
bicycle	male	nickel
bottle	module	panel
buckle	muscle	parallel

German gave the English language words such as *quartz, liverwurst, dachshund, pumpernickel,* and *schnitzel.*

76

-*le* (cont.)		-*el* (cont.)
cable	people	squirrel
cattle	rubble	travel
circle	simple	tunnel
comfortable	table	
couple	tackle	

Students will notice from this list that -*able* words end in-*le*; if not, their attention should be drawn to this. You could provide these lists and prompt students to add to them. They will also note that their odds of being right will be better if they put -*le* instead of -*el* at the end of a word.

Further study of the -le ending: You may want students to notice that after a short vowel, they double the consonant, and then add -*le*. Creating a list to verify this guiding principle could look like this:

apple	kettle	middle	bottle	bubble
babble	settle	giggle	toggle	muddle
battle	embezzle	riddle	topple	struggle
saddle	nettle	ripple	throttle	snuggle
straddle		scribble	hobble	cuddle
dazzle		nibble		puddle
raffle		little		juggle

Don't Forget -al

Words also end in -*al*, but there are fewer of them than those ending in -*le*.

Students could generate a list of common words ending in -*al* that they use in their writing. Among them might be *animal, capital, cereal, electrical, historical,* and *mammal.* Still, -*le* is by far the most common ending of -*able*, -*ckle*, and -*le* and more common than -*el* and -*al* altogether.

Students who are used to looking for patterns could decide to take the -*le* ending a step further and explore words ending in -*ckle*, as in *tackle, crackle, heckle, freckle, tickle, pickle, buckle, chuckle,* and *knuckle.* Or, they may decide that certain groupings work better for them, and that's just fine. The goal is to help them remember that -*le* is the dominant ending.

Word Thief: A Game on Word Origins

Since French and languages of Germanic origin (e.g., Old Norse) are major contributors to English words, and since the English went to great lengths to communicate with their European neighbors, students may want to play Word Thief, a game related to word origins and spellings. Before playing this game, though, much practice in creating word patterns and working with word origins will be needed. The idea, though, is that students will learn more about word origins as they play. If, for example, a student makes a note that *staple* does not fit under the white flag for Other because he thought it ended in -*el*, he now knows it belongs with the French flag and ends in -*le*.

The game requires four or five players, with each having two small flags — French and German — and one white rectangle. The two flags are held up to denote the country the word came from, and the white rectangle is for words that don't fit. For example, for *circle*, which is French in origin, a player would hold up a French flag, whereas for *hazel*, which lacks the French -*le* ending, a player would hold up a white flag. Some guessing will occur, but students will also hear words spelled aloud correctly.

The teacher or moderator reads out the words, and the first person to hold up the correct flag from the country of origin earns one point. If that player can spell the word correctly, he or she will gain two more points. If the word is misspelled, then one person is chosen by the moderator to spell the word and will get two

---

points for a correct answer. The points gained by each player are noted on an honor system. If no one can spell the word correctly, then the moderator spells it and returns that word to the game. The person to reach 21 first wins, calls out "Word Thief," and then chooses to become the moderator or to continue playing. The game then begins again.

A game sheet sample for the moderator is provided, but as students learn more about words and origins, they can create their own sheet for the game. Students can adapt the game, if they wish, to include words from other languages, as long as they know where the words originated; they can also indicate something that makes the words identifiable (e.g., that they are everyday words or words with a particular ending).

German Flag (Old Norse words, which have Germanic roots, and relate to the every day)	French Flag	White Flag (Other: Words ending in -el)
bag	little	hazel
cake	staple	squirrel
egg	bicycle	nickel
hug	cable	travel
kid	angle	tunnel
leg	table	camel
root	simple	funnel
scale	bottle	pixel
seat	kettle	jewel
sister	circle	marvel
skin	buckle	hotel
skirt	bubble	barrel
sky	puzzle	panel
Thursday	couple	travel
window	garage	
wing	mirage	
birth	collage	

Idiomatic Phrases

As well as finding interest and meaning in the words that entered English over many centuries, it is necessary to look at words that do not adhere to literal meaning. Including them as you build word knowledge is important as they are difficult to understand for many students, particularly those who are bilingual and trilingual, and who might take them literally. Idiomatic phrases provide a great way to have fun with words, as well. Better still, they lend themselves to great punchlines for jokes and link to word narratives because you can create stories about them.

Sometimes, you can suggest that students find idiomatic expressions on a theme.

Many picture books have fun with idiomatic expressions. Students may want to check the school library and public library for collections. Some recommended titles:

- *The Cat's Pajamas* by Wallace Edwards
- *The World Is Your Oyster* by Tamara James
- *Out of the Blue* by Vanita Oelschlager
- *Birds of a Feather* by Vanita Oelschlager

Picture books provide a hilarious source of idiom illustrations, which engage and amuse, and may inspire children to create their own illustrated book of idioms, with the sequel being a book of idiom jokes.

Students can begin to create several lists of idioms and add to them as they come across idiomatic expressions. This study would benefit by beginning with wordplay and jokes such as the following:

"Why are idioms like good jokes?"
"They both have punch lines!"

"Why did the children skip gym class? "
"They were tired of jumping rope!"

Students could then collect sets of idiomatic expressions, such as those below, adding phrases to their lists as they read books, search websites, and ask others, including parents. Here are a few sets of expressions:

- *bird* idioms, such as bird brain, nest egg, egghead, keeping an eagle eye on someone, taking a person under the wing, or wondering why a little bird told someone a secret
- *cold* idioms, such as cold comfort, getting cold feet, getting the cold shoulder, staying out of the cold, or being killed in cold blood
- *beat* idioms, such as beat about the bushes, beat up, beat off (an attack or an attacker), beat the drum (to create support for something), beat down (as in reducing a price to make a bargain), and off the beaten track (in a remote place)
- *foot* idioms, as in drag one's feet, find one's feet, get a foot in the door, get cold feet, get off on the wrong foot, not put a foot wrong, put one's best foot forward, put one's foot down, put one's foot in it, sweep someone off their feet, and think on one's feet

Once students are more familiar with idioms, they could create jokes along these lines:

"Why did the husband buy a broom? "
"He wanted to sweep his wife off her feet."

"Why was the old man afraid to buy new socks? "
"He suffered from cold feet!"

The jokes will improve as students engage in wordplay and become better aware of idioms.

As more than 10 000 idioms exist, it should be possible for students to devise questions like these on their own. They may want to create a PowerPoint or Prezi presentation, selecting appropriate photographs for their jokes. As they live in a world of media, they are usually highly motivated when using any kind of web tool.

It is especially important to introduce idiomatic phrases to English Language Learners. They, like many other children, tend to take the phrases literally. For students, a possible Internet source is www.myenglishpages.com, and for teachers or older students, a good site to check out is www.idiomconnection.com (as there are idioms listed from A to Z, plus lists of animal, bird, clothing, food, heart, money, and other idioms). Students will undoubtedly find others.

Idiomatic phrases could be grouped together to study. For example, students could consider animal idioms such as these:

herding cats	having a frog in your throat
letting the cat out of the bag	monkey business
playing cat and mouse	making a pig of yourself
to chicken out of something	having a whale of a time
elephant in the room	crying wolf

One Idiom, Several Cross-Cultural Versions

The idiom "raining cats and dogs" has inspired many imaginative explanations on the Internet and elsewhere. One interesting, but unconfirmed notion is that old English houses had thatched roofs and the animals liked to sleep on them; however, during heavy rains, they were washed away, so it seemed to be "raining cats and dogs."

Many countries have unusual-sounding expressions for rain, and students may be interested in researching these. The source of my examples below is www.omniglot.com/language/idioms/. I recommend this site for teachers because it features many languages with idioms translated into English.

Afrikaans — "It's raining old women with knobkerries." (clubs)

Bulgarian, Croatian, Latvian, Serbian, and Russian — "It's raining from a bucket."

Danish — "it's raining shoemakers' apprentices."

French — "It's raining frogs [or nails or buckets]."

Greek — "It's raining chair legs."

Norwegian — "It's raining trolls."

On New Year's Eve in 2010, however, about 3000 blackbirds and starlings did fall from the sky in Beebe, Arkansas. High winds in the area were given as the explanation. No cats and dogs were reported to have fallen!

Knowing What to Make of Prefixes and Suffixes

No one expects students to know the origin of every word in English, but some origins would help them with spelling. For example, knowledge of Latin- and Greek-based prefixes and suffixes is particularly useful.

Common Latin prefixes

re means "again"	Definition
rebuild	to build again
reboot (a computer)	to boot or start again
reappear	to appear again
revisit	to visit again

pre means "before"	Definition
pretest	to test beforehand
prehistoric	before recorded history
prepay	pay before due, or pay ahead of time
pre-exist	exist before

co means "together" or "with"	Definition
co-author	author or write together
co-edit	edit together
coexist	exist with
co-pilot	pilot with
coteach	teach together

Students should be able to work out meanings of the words, when given the meaning of the prefix.

More prefixes of Latin origin

Here is a selection of other prefixes that students may find helpful.

Latin Prefix	English Examples
inter means "between"	interlock, intercom, interstate, interface
in means "not"	insane, inhuman, incapable
il means "not"	illegal, illogical, illiterate
im means "not"	impossible, immature, impersonal
ir means "not"	irregular, irrational

Latin Prefix	English Examples
non means "not" or "no"	non-smoking, non-fiction, nonsense
sub means "under" or "below"	subway, submarine, subterranean
trans means "across" or "through"	transatlantic, transport, transect

Greek prefixes

Greek prefixes are less common. Here are a few accompanied by English words that use them.

Greek Prefix	English Examples
hyper means "over" or "excessive"	hyperactive, hyperdrive
palin means "backwards"	palindrome (e.g., dad, pop, mom)
sym or *syn* means "with" or "together"	sympathy; synonym
tele means "far" or "at a distance"	telephone, television, telecast, teleconference, telephoto, telescope
auto means "self"	autobiography, automobile, autofocus
hemi means "half" or "partially"	hemisphere
multi means "many"	multiplication, multicolored, multilingual, multicultural
tri means "three" (same in Latin)	triangle, tripod, trisect

Knowing the prefix *tele-* prevents the common mistake of "telivision," which is related to hearing the sound /i/ instead of recognizing the prefix *tele-* plus base word.

Using prefix knowledge to help spell

I would predict that what is most useful for spelling words with a prefix is to question whether to double a consonant or not. For example, the prefix *mis-* came from German into English, but how does knowing this prefix help with spelling? Well, if the prefix *mis-* is at the beginning of a word, there will be only one *s*, as in *misbehave*, since *mis-* plus the base word *behave* makes *misbehave*. The only variance will be when the base word starts with *s* and the prefix ends in *s*. For example, *mis-* plus *spell* equals *misspell* — one of the most commonly misspelled words in English! Similarly, if students know the prefix *il-*, they know that *il-* plus *legal* equals *illegal*. The same process applies for *irregular* because it consists of the prefix *ir* plus *regular*. Understanding this pattern should help in the spelling of many words. The only word I can think of in which you can spell the root word and the prefix, but the meaning does not work is *flammable* because when you add *in-* to *flammable* to get *inflammable*, the meaning remains the same! We need to use *non-flammable* or *fireproof* to create the opposite meaning. Other words, such as *regular* and *irregular* and *legal* and *illegal*, conform. Students may consider investigating if there are any other exceptions, or if 99 percent of words follow this rule.

Checking for affixes

Students may wish to keep a list of common prefixes and check for them in their writing. They could also begin a table like the ones above and list examples of words they use that have prefixes. They can then add this to an editing checklist and apply it when they edit. Here is a sample checklist, which notes both a few word endings and prefixes.

I can edit by ...	List or comment
checking for -al and -el endings, and listing -el words	squirrel, parallel
listing words ending in -al that I use	animal, digital
looking for words with prefixes, such as dis-, pre-, co-, and tele-	"Now I get **tele**vision correct every time!"

Common suffixes

Just as knowledge of prefixes can help students to become more successful spellers, so can knowledge of suffixes. When students learn more about suffixes, they can use this information to inform their spelling. It is therefore reasonable to begin with the four most common suffixes. As Bill Honig, Linda Diamond, and Linda Gutlohn note in *Teaching Reading Sourcebook: For Kindergarten Through Eighth Grade*, the suffixes -ed, -ing, -ly, and -s/es account for 97 percent of words with suffixes in printed school English.

Suffix	Meaning	Examples
-ed	used to make past tense of verbs	jumped, waited, walked
-ing	verb, participle	jumping, waiting, walking
-ly	characteristic of, used to make adverbs	brightly, loudly, happily
-s, -es	more than one, used to make plurals	bags, locks; buses, foxes

Beginning with these common suffixes is key since it is highly likely that students use these endings. Students can easily look for them in their writing. As they become more informed, they can begin to self-correct.

For example, when my daughter was very young, I decided to share with her that every time she heard the sound /ing/, she could write *ing*, so that evening she wrote "pingk" for *pink*. It would have been helpful if I had added "when you hear /ing/ *at the end of a word.*" Because I read to her daily, she loved to play with words, and at an early age, she wrote amazing poetry. She was motivated to record her work, but at that point she was much more concerned with creating the writing than with spelling the words accurately. As she grew older, editing became more important, depending on audience. Although I shared information on spelling with her, we really focused on books and authors. So as she grew older, she became a lover of words, a prolific reader, and an excellent writer, which was truly my goal for her. As teachers and parents, we want to create writers who want to write, who are able to edit and self-correct spelling, not spellers who don't care to write!

Knowing that -*ly* is a suffix helps greatly with spelling. Instead of wondering about doubling consonants, spellers can add -*ly* to an adjective to form an adverb.

Base Word — Noun	Adjective	Adverb
beauty	beautiful	beautiful**ly**
care	careful	careful**ly**
anxiety	anxious	anxious**ly**
courage	courageous	courageous**ly**
dream	dreamy	dreami**ly**
doubt	doubtful	doubtful**ly**

Base Word — Adjective	Adverb
dim	dim**ly**
brisk	brisk**ly**
bright	bright**ly**
equal	equal**ly**
happy	happi**ly**
joyful	joyful**ly**

Students can work with the teacher to keep track of their use of adverbs that end in -*ly* and remind themselves that they are just adding a suffix; hence, *equal* plus -*ly* equals *equally*. They also need to know that if the word ends in -*y*, as in *happy*, then they change the *y* to *i* before adding -*ly*, as in *happily*. Such information would be shared in small groups in mini-lessons related to students' writing.

Suffixes related to comparison

Adding -*er* or -*est* to adjectives — for example, *small, smaller, smallest* — is done so that nouns can be compared according to degree. For example, consider these sentences: To climb Mount Everest is much hard**er** than climbing Mount Washington. Amy is short**er** than Chawa, but Ashley is the short**est**.

Here is a chant to remind students of what to do.

It would be good for students to create a chant of their own, related to this topic.

It's all about degree —
and very clear to me!
You add *e, r,* or *e, s, t,*
for more and most, you see!
You can be *sad, sadder,*
or *saddest* of all.
The sky can be *dark, darker,*
or *darkest.*
You can be *quick, quicker,*
or *quickest* of all.
You can be *smart, smarter,*
or *smartest*!

For most words, *-er* or *-est* is added when needed, and it is comforting to know this; as students learn more about these suffixes, however, they will discover that there are some exceptions to adding these comparative endings. It would be helpful for students to record them, as they come across them in their reading or writing. For example, we would not say "deliciouser, deliciousest"; instead, we would say "more delicious, most delicious." Similarly, we would say "more exciting, most exciting" and "more difficult, most difficult." Students will recognize that "difficulter," for example, just sounds wrong, and it is! They need to know that the word *more* is substituted for *-er* and *most* for *-est*. They also need to be aware of words that change in comparison, as in *good, better, best*, and *bad, worse, worst*; however, these are few.

Common suffixes

Some suffixes that students will find useful to know and be exposed to, over time, are listed in the table below. Mini-lessons would be the best way to present them. Students can explore words with these suffixes and investigate how these create endings for many words.

Suffix	Examples
-er, -or — someone who does this	writer, editor
-tion — act, process, used to make nouns	attraction, subtraction, correction
-able, -ible — able to be, can be	agreeable, digestible
-al — having this characteristic; used to make adjectives	musical, additional, arrival
-ful means "full of, characterized by," "able to," and "as much as will fill"	careful, helpful, thankful, thoughtful wakeful, harmful, spoonful
-ness — means "full of," used to make nouns	kind, kindness; happy, happiness; quiet, quietness
-ous, -ious — having qualities of, full of; used to make adjectives	dangerous, mountainous, hazardous studious, luxurious
-y — characterized by, used to make adjectives	cream, creamy; wit, witty; noise, noisy; fog, foggy; ice, icy; mist, misty; rock, rocky, cloud, cloudy
-ly — means "like in appearance"; "characterized by how often something is done"; used to make adjectives into adverbs; and nouns into adjectives	fatherly, smoothly hourly, weekly, monthly bad, badly; loud, loudly; correct, correctly; wrong, wrongly friend, friendly; beast, beastly; hill, hilly
-less means "lacking"	careless, thoughtless, friendless
-er, -est — more, most	bigger, biggest; taller, tallest; shorter, shortest; longer, longest

With the suffix *-ly*, students should begin to notice that they simply add *-ly* to the base word. Exceptions occur only when the word ends with two *l*'s, as in *hill, hilly; full, fully*. No words in English have three consecutive *l*'s, so no terrain should ever be "hillly," and no one should comment that a project is not "fullly" funded!

Developmental Journey Review

Teachers assess where students are on the journey to becoming knowledgeable word users and informed word constructors. As the chart below reminds us, in the left-column, we can see where students begin this journey. As we reflect on what students know of sound or visual appearance, function, and meaning patterns, we may be able to identify possible gaps in their knowledge.

This review chart goes from easier to more difficult.

Pattern by Sound/ Visual Appearance (Graphophonic)	Pattern by Function (Syntactic)	Pattern by Meaning (Semantic)
the knowledge that the alphabet names stay constant, but sounds change	base words	wordplay (e.g., puns, riddles, jokes)
single consonant sounds, then blends (e.g., *bl, gl, spl*)	verb endings (e.g., *-ed, -ing*)	prefixes (as they relate to base words)
short vowel patterns (using anchor words on a word wall to create patterns (e.g., *run, fun*)	plurals	suffixes (as they relate to base words)
long vowel patterns (including *rimes*, which sound the same and are visually similar (e.g., t*ake*, f*ake*) and *rhymes*, which simply have the same sound pattern (*eight, ate*)	contractions (and simple possessives)	word origins
vowel pairs with choices (e.g., *oi* or *oy* — *oy* is usually at the end of words)	compound words (hyphen or no hyphen; separate or together?)	word narratives related to origin
silent letters (related to letters that have sound, e.g., crum**b**, crum**ble** — visual link is also key here)	adjectives	idioms
vowels plus *r*	adverbs	similes, metaphors, and other literary devices (e.g., alliteration and hyperbole)

In early grades, sound patterns are a base, followed by function patterns, and finally, by meaning patterns. Although "vowels plus *r*" is in the sound column, it is one of the most difficult sound patterns; in Grades 4 through 6, students are likely better able to distinguish between *bird, her,* and *fur*.

Students need to notice, question, and closely examine words, as they constantly form and test hypotheses about how words are spelled. Much word knowledge has to be built so that students learn about meaning patterns, including word origins, word narratives, prefixes, and suffixes. As they learn through mini-lessons, writer's workshop, peer editing, investigations, the creation of word narratives, and wordplay, students are better able to make informed predictions. They continue to study, probe, and question the construction, derivation, and meaning of words. Through observing student learning, teachers will be able to assess how well they are growing in their word and spelling knowledge and how well they are applying this to their writing.

Vowel plus *r*

When a vowel is followed by *r*, it makes a special sound and often causes trouble with spelling. It may be helpful for students to know that *ar* usually sounds like the /ar/ in *car* or *star* and *or* usually sounds like the /or/ in *for* or *fork*. The problem lies with *ir, er,* and *ur*, as they often sound the same. Here, reliance has to move away from sound to visual and pattern links, where *bird* is taught with *third*, and *girl* with *whirl*. In longer words "using vowels plus *r*," usually the suffix *-er* is the most common ending (e.g., *hotter, warmer, teacher, winner*). Students can check to see if this is true when they check word endings while reading and writing.

6

Spelling Rules

There are many spelling rules, and people are quick to point out exceptions to these rules. What is not widely appreciated is that most of these rules hold true 80 percent of the time. Since spelling is an interactive language process, where students constantly test to verify, rules are best used as a trigger to inquiry.

Ten Common Rules

1. There is at least one vowel (*a, e, i, o, u*) in every syllable.

Consider, for example, *buffalo, halo, potato, library,* and *story*. The vowel is sometimes *y*. This rule holds true 100 percent of the time; however, students still have to look out for double vowels in single syllables, as in *soar, dear,* and *spoil*.

2. *i* before *e* except after *c* — or when sounding like /ay/.

This rule works most of the time (about 90 percent):

> *i* before *e,* as in *friend, field, shield, thief, chief, belief, believe, piece, priest*
> **except** after *c,* as in *receive, deceive, ceiling, perceive, conceit*
> or when sounding like /ay/, as in *neighbor* and *weigh.*

Other words that have a long /a/ sound and follow the rule include these: *beige, dreidel, eight, eighty, eighteen, veil, reign, rein, their,* and *weight*. Students can probably find more. Prompt them to collect words related to the rule.

It is important to emphasize words that follow the rule *i* before *e* except after *c* and to have students list words that they discover are exceptions to it, for example, *science, conscience, ancient, species, sufficient,* and *society.*

I predict that if students apply this rule, their spelling of words with *ie* or *ei* combinations will be completely accurate if they record the few exceptions they use and check for them as they edit.

> There are also words with *ei* not following *c* and not sounding like /ay/. These include *weird, seize, protein, caffeine, either, neither, eiderdown, Fahrenheit, forfeit, height,* and *leisure.*

3. After a short vowel, double the consonant.

The pattern is consonant, vowel, consonant, or C V C. This rule applies to words of more than one syllable, for example,

> happy, rabbit, better, yellow, silly, sorry, hurry, letter

Exception: *k* is never doubled; instead, use *ck*, as in these words: *blacker, jacket, cracking, checking, chicken, cricket, sticky, pocket, lucky.* *Soccer* sounds as if it has a double *k*, but is, of course, spelled with *cc*.

Remember, too, that *x* and *v* are not doubled, with these exceptions: *revved* and *savvy*.

Finding words that have single and double consonants, and are somewhat difficult to spell would be another list, including, for example, these:

accelerate, broccoli, Caribbean, difference, magically
necessary, official, parallel, raspberry, tomorrow

4. Words of one syllable that end in *f, l,* or *s* double the last letter after a short vowel.

Students would need to judge how useful this rule might be, but it is worthy of an investigation. The following chant might serve as a jumping-off point.

F L S Rule
Short words that end
In *f, l,* or *s,*
Double last letters —
YES! YES! YES!
Staff and *stiff,*
And *grill* and *still,*
Floss and *gloss,*
And *will* and *fill,*
Mess and *chess,*
And *yell* and *tell,*
Follow the pattern
Fairly well.
Except for *yes* —
One *s,* I guess!

Because we would be asking students to verify this rule by generating lists of words, I am providing some words they might find in their search. Note that these words are all short. Longer words tend to have a single letter *l* — for example, *beautiful, helpful, fanciful* — because the suffix *-ful* is spelled with one *l*.

F L S Word List
F: staff, stiff, stuff, cliff, bluff, cuff, fluff, gruff, huff, muff, sniff, scuff, off

L: all, ball, shall, small, fall, call, hall, mall, stall, squall, tall, wall
bell, cell, fell, sell, shell, spell, swell, tell, well, yell,
ill, bill, chill, drill, fill, frill, gill, grill, hill, kill, mill, pill, quill, shrill, still, skill, spill, till, thrill, will
doll, scroll, toll, roll, poll, stroll
bull, dull, gull, hull, lull, mull, pull, skull

S: bass, lass, mass, pass
chess, cress, guess, less, mess, press
hiss, kiss, miss
boss, floss, gloss, loss, toss
fuss

Unlike Rule 3, which applies to words of more than one syllable, Rule 4 applies to words of only one syllable, ending in *f, l,* or *s.*

Exceptions: yes, of, us, bus, gas, if, pal

5. Most plurals follow rules, at least 80 percent of the time.

See Chapter 3 for more details on plurals.

Plurals in English refers to "more than one." There are three common ways to make plurals: by adding *s*, by adding *es*, and by changing *y* to *i* and adding *es*.

a) The most common way to make a singular word into a plural is to add *-s*. Students could investigate the list of words for which this holds true, for example:

> cat, cats; dog, dogs; frog, frogs; bat, bats;
> mat, mats; shop, shops; car, cars; cow, cows

As they make a list, you could point out that words ending in *g* like *dog* still add an *s* to make it plural, although it sounds like /z/.

b) The next common plural ending is *-es*. The good news is that students can hear the *-es* ending so it is quite easy for them to get it correct. Examples:

> box, boxes; fox, foxes; tax, taxes;
> peach, peaches; church, churches; hutch, hutches

c) Change *y* to *i* and add *-es* in these instances:
If a word ends with a vowel plus *y*, simply add *s*. Examples:

> boy, boys; toy, toys, key, keys; monkey, monkeys; holiday, holidays

If a word ends in a consonant plus *y*, change the *y* to *i*, and add *es*. Examples:

> baby, babies; family, families; diary, diaries;
> factory, factories; allergy, allergies

There are some exceptions to these three endings, but they do not put much burden on memory, and many students already know the common ones, these among them:

> man, men; woman, women; child, children; goose, geese;
> tooth, teeth; foot, feet; person, people; mouse, mice; die, dice

For Advanced Spellers
The following sets of less common words could be added much later, as students discover or use them: *louse* and *lice*, *cactus* and *cacti*, *radius* and *radii*, *octopus* and *octopi*, *alumnus* and *alumni*, *index* and *indices*, *crisis* and *crises*, *vortex* and *vortices*, *vertex* and *vertices*.

The best part is that students need to know how to spell only the words they use. So, from the list above, their top usage words would be *men*, *women*, and *people*. That puts little pressure on their memories or on the list of exceptions they start to make.

6. When you add *all* or *full* to a word or syllable, you drop an *l*.

Examples:

> **all** — always, almost, already, also
> **full** — hopeful, dreadful, grateful, helpful, painful, fulfill, joyful

You may want to point out to students that when they change *hopeful* into an adverb, they are not doubling the *l*; instead, they are adding the suffix *-ly* to make *hopefully*.

Similarly, *till* becomes *until*. (In British English, however, the *l* in *distill* and *instill* is doubled.)

7. *e*, *i*, and *y* soften the sound of the letters *c* and *g*.

Examples:

Hard *c*: cat, cut   Soft *c*: city, cycle
Hard *g*: gang, gum   Soft *g*: gentle, giant

ce	ci	cy
ice	city	cycle
cell	pencil	cygnet [baby swan]
centre	circus	cyclamen
place	citizen	lacy
office	racing	Lucy

ge	gi	gy
gem	giant	energy
age	ginger	biology
danger	magic	gymnastics
gentle	giraffe	sociology
dungeon	tragic	gyrate

Students might find it interesting to add to these lists and to develop the following list, where *u* is inserted after *g* to keep the /g/ hard:

guide, guilt, guitar, disguise, guess, guest, rogue

This relationship makes sense of an "odd" spelling.

There are only a few exceptions to this rule — *get, give, girl,* and *begin* among them — but they are often spelled correctly, so it is better not to list them; however, *girl* is often spelled "gril," and so the word has to be memorized and listed in a pattern with *whirl, twirl,* and *swirl*.

8. After a short vowel that is followed by a /ch/ sound, put *t* before *ch*.

Remind students that a short vowel is the sound the letter makes, as /a/ in *cat*, /e/ in *bell*, /i/ in *bit*, /o/ in *lot*, and /u/ in *cut*.

catch	stretch	ditch	notch	Dutch
hatch	fetch	pitch	botch	hutch
match	ketchup	kitchen	blotch	crutch

batch	wretch	stitch	splotch	clutch
latch	etch	itch	butterscotch	
patch	sketch	hitch	hopscotch	

This rule works about 90 percent of the time. The only exceptions in words of one syllable are *much*, *rich*, *which*, and *such*. In multi-syllable words, exceptions include *ostrich*, *duchess*, *sandwich*, *attach*, and *bachelor*.

9. After a short vowel that is followed by a /ge/ sound, put *d* before *ge*.

badge	edge	ridge	dodge	fudge
badger	hedge	bridge	lodger	judge
gadget	ledge	fridge	dislodge	nudge
	dredge	cartridge	hodgepodge	begrudge
	hedgehog	drawbridge	mislodge	budge
	pledge	fidget		budget
	knowledge	footbridge		sludge
	sledge	partridge		trudge
	wedge	porridge		

No *d* follows if there is another consonant after the vowel, as in *plunge* and *bulge*.

Exceptions to the "-dge rule" happen in some multi-syllable words ending in *-age* or *-ege*: *village*, *cottage*, *garbage*; *college*, *privilege*; however, more words follow the rule than not.

In *-nge* words, the /a/ is long, so no *d* is needed: *range*, *change*, *stranger*, *danger*, *angel*.

In regular long-vowel /a/ words, no *d* is needed before *-ge*, for example:

cage, rage, page, sage, stage, age, agent, danger, engage

The word *privilege* is commonly misspelled with a *d*.

10. When you hear /chur/ at the end of a word, write *-ture*.

Examples:

picture, nature, culture, creature, feature

Students can investigate this ending and add to the list above. Remind them that they should never write "chur."

Putting the rules in context

The 10 spelling rules outlined above, as well as the information on adding -*ing,* are better treated as guidelines than as rules. Encourage students to use them only if they find them helpful during editing. A possible editing checklist to grow out of consideration of the guidelines might look like this:

When I edit, I will consider these questions:	Check
Do I check that every syllable has a vowel or *y*?	
Did the rule *i* before *e* except after *c* help me when initially writing words or while editing?	
After short vowels, do I remember to double the consonant?	
When forming plurals, do I add *s* or *es*, or change *y* to *i* and add *es*?	

Investigating the Strength of Rules

Using rules as guidelines or generalizations is probably a better way to regard them, as we think of rules as immutable but generalizations as things that apply most of the time. There is enough variation in the rules that students would benefit from making investigations so that they discover word patterns on their own and create generalizations to share.

Initially, it would be useful if the generalizations students explored worked almost 100 percent of the time. For example, an investigation with regard to the sound /kw/ might be expressed in the following way.

Q: "How is the sound /kw/ most commonly spelled in English?"

Students should find that the answer is *qu* except for advertising signs such as "Kwik Print," which are intended to attract attention. They might come across the words *Kwanza*, a festival, and *kwacha*, a currency used in Zambia and Malawi. A rare exception would be *choir*. In identifying the main way the /kw/ sound is made, students will find that the letter *q* is always followed by *u* as in *queen*, *quickly*, and *quiet*, but that no words, except some of Arabic origin as in *Iraq*, end with *q*.

Generalization to share: When you hear the sound /kw/ in English, you write *qu*.

A possible follow-up question: "What do you notice about words containing *qu* and a short /o/ sound, as in *squash*, *squabble*, *quality*, *qualify*, and *quarter*?" Students will quickly notice that these words are spelled *qua*. They might come up with this generalization: When you hear the sound /kw/ in English, followed by a short /o/ sound, you write *qua*.

Q: "Do single syllable words with a short vowel end in *-ck* or *-c* or *-k*?"

My findings were that only three single-syllable words with short vowels end in *-c*, and depending on how you pronounce *chic*, maybe only two — *disc* and *sac* (as in embryonic sac). Few words end in *-k*, one being *trek*; all others have a second consonant before *-k*: *aardvark, park, ark, ask, hawk, work, blank, think, mark, milk, desk, elk, link, pink*. Instead of telling students this, encourage them to make note of it. They will then become keen observers of words and letters.

Many words follow the pattern of the spelling *-ck* when the /k/ sound follows a short vowel. Here are some of them.

back	check	brick	clock	buck
black	deck	chick	crock	cluck
clack	fleck	click	dock	duck
crack	heck	flick	flock	luck
hack	neck	lick	knock	muck
jack	peck	pick	lock	puck
lack	speck	quick	mock	suck
knack	wreck	sick	rock	stuck
pack		slick	sock	tuck
rack		stick	shock	truck
sack		tick	stock	yuck
slack		thick		
smack		trick		
snack		wick		
track				

Do More Words Begin with *c* or with *k*?

If students explore this question, they may be interested to discover that more words begin with *c*, as in *camp*, than with *k*, as in *kangaroo*; occasionally, words begin with hard /ch/, as in *chasm, character, chorus, chameleon, chemical*, and *chord*.

This finding still holds true when you add -*y*, as in *lucky, sticky, tricky, rocky*; or when you add the suffix -*ly*, as in *quickly, sickly, thickly*.

Generalization to share: When you hear the sound /k/ in words of one syllable after a short vowel, you write *ck*.

Words of more than one syllable ending in the sound /k/ are more complex, but therefore interesting to investigate.

Q: "Do more multi-syllable words end in -*c* or -*ck*?"

Findings will be interesting, but I predict that students will discover the following:

- Although more than 500 multi-syllable words end in -*ck*, the common ones are nearly all compound words. Students may list words such as the following:

  airsick, applejack, armlock, backpack, backtrack, bedrock, bodycheck, bookrack, bottleneck, breadstick, broomstick, candlestick, crewneck, cutback, drawback, drumstick, feedback, flapjack, hardback, knapsack, lipstick, outback, quarterback, roadblock, seasick, shipwreck, slapstick, soundtrack, starstruck, sunblock, woodchuck

- If a multi-syllable word ends with the sound /ick/, then the suffix is -*ic* and it is spelled that way at the end of the word. These words would be adjectives. The suffix -*ic* means "characteristic of or pertaining to." Students may list words such as the following:

  allergic, athletic, basic, bionic, classic, cosmetic, cubic, democratic, electric, fantastic, idiotic, microscopic, optimistic, pathetic, poetic, realistic, sarcastic, scientific, specific, terrific, toxic, tragic

There are also nouns that end in -*ic*:

  Arctic, antic, attic, clinic, logic, magic, panic, traffic

Generalizations to share:

If a multi-syllable word ends in the sound /ick/ and it is a compound word, it is usually spelled -*ck*.

If a multi-syllable word ends in the sound /ick/ and it is an adjective, the ending is usually spelled -*ic*.

These examples are just around different /k/ sounds at the beginnings and ends of words, but there are many more possibilities. Take a look at other letters at the beginnings and ends of words. For example, you might have students investigate the following question.

Q: "When *w* is at the end of a word, is it always preceded by a vowel, as in *cow* and *now*?"

Students will find words such as *arrow, burrow, borrow, crow, grow, throw, row, scarecrow, sparrow,* and *wheelbarrow,* which may help them when spelling some words they would be tempted to end with *o*. Having looked at a vowel plus *w*

A few multi-syllable words end in -*ac*, something that could prompt a short investigation. Students might come up with these words: *cardiac, lilac, iMac, shellac, tarmac, zodiac.*

The ending -*oc* is also rare. The only common word I could find was *havoc*. There are also abbreviations such as *croc* and *doc*.

at the end of words, students could consider *w* plus a vowel at the beginning of words such as these:

> was, want, water, watch, wash, wander, war, warm,
> ward, wart, warble, warrant

Many young students say "woz" for *was* and spell it "wos" or "woz." Since *was* is a commonly misspelled word, the generalization about writing *wa* might be helpful to many students.

Ask, "When you hear /w/ and a short /o/), what do you write?"

It is easy to make this generalization: that when you hear /w/ plus short /o/ at the beginning of a word, you write *wa*.

Students would be able to add words they use to create a list such as this one:

> wad, waddle, waffle, walk, wallaby, wallop, walrus, wampum, warped,
> Warsaw, washroom, wasp, waterfall, watermark, watermelon, watt

The only exceptions I can find to this are *wobble*, along with its derivatives *wobbly* and *wobbled*, and *wok*.

Similarly, you can lead students to investigate the following question.

Q: "When you hear words starting with *w* and the short /u/ sound, what do you write?"

The list students develop might look like this:

> won, wonder, worry, work, word, world, worm, worth, worthy, worse

Students could then make this hypothesis: When we hear words starting with the sound /w/ and the short /u/ sound, we write *wo*.

Other words that have the sound of short /u/ but are written with an *o* are *monk*, *money*, *honey*, and *come*.

"Come and listen, come and listen, to the robins as they work, Who would doubt that they are worthy of the worms they pull from dirt?"

You may want to encourage students to write a few lines of poetry incorporating some of the words that follow the generalization. (A sample appears in the margin.) To do this, they would create a list of words supporting the hypothesis and then create one or two rhyming couplets, including a few of the list words. Tell them to highlight the list words in some way. A good idea for this activity is to have students work in pairs.

Another investigation, this time related to endings, could grow out of the following question.

Q: "When you hear the sound /f/ at the end of a word, how is it spelled?"

Right away, students will think of the words *of* and *if*, although a Grade 2 student once told me that *of* was spelled "ov." "Listen to the sound," he said. "Ov!" He was eventually persuaded that sound did not always determine the way a word was spelled.

If you remind students of single syllable words with the double *ff* rule, they should be able to generate a list, as in *cuff, staff, stiff, cliff, stuff, huff, puff, bluff, fluff, gruff, scruff,* and *off*.

Photograph could be a word for a riddle, as it has *ph* at both ends.

Then comes the problem: they think of a word like *graph*, and they have a whole new pattern:

> autogra**ph**, **ph**otogra**ph**, paragra**ph**, epita**ph**, choreogra**ph**

There could also be a list with *ph* within the word creating an /f/ sound:

> Geogra**ph**y, **ph**otogra**ph**y, al**ph**abet, hy**ph**en, ele**ph**ant,
> ne**ph**ew, gra**ph**ics, em**ph**asis, am**ph**ibian, pam**ph**let,
> **ph**rase, para**ph**rase, biogra**ph**y, atmos**ph**ere, meta**ph**or

Students will need to know only the words they use in writing, but they do need to know that *ph* is an alternative spelling for the sound /f/.

Less frequently used is the spelling *gh* to make an /f/ sound, as in *laugh, laughter, cough, enough, tough, rough,* and *trough,* but it is the final alternative spelling of /f/.

Possible generalization: When you hear the sound /f/, you write *f* or *ff,* and sometimes *ph*.

Promoting Wondering About Words

It matters less what words and patterns students investigate as that they *do* investigate them, notice them, wonder about them, and share their findings with the teacher and with one another. Inquiry becomes a constant when students begin to look at words and word patterns in this way.

Assessing *never, always, most*

One way to promote inquiry is to present students with a variety of statements and ask them to either find proof for them or qualify how accurate they are. Invite them to assess whether the generalizations they determine are helpful to them as they edit.

Never:
- Never write *s h u n* at the end of a word. (The most common ending for that sound is *-tion*.)
- Never end a word with *j, v,* or *q*. (Students may find *rev* and *Iraq*, an Arabian word, to refute this. They may then want to alter the phrase to "Most of the time words don't end in *j, v,* or *q*." However, it can help them edit quickly if they have written "hav" or other words where they have left off an *e* which was supposed to follow *v*.)
- Never write *kk*. (Use *ck* instead.)
- Never write *vv*. (But you can do so if writing *revved*.)

Students may enjoy coming up with more of these statements or amending them to "Most of the time . . ."

Always:
Students can also be asked to create statements, such as the Always statements below.

- Always remember that every syllable has a vowel (*a, e, i, o, u*), or *y*.
- Always use *-dge* after short vowels and *-ge* after long vowels. (Examples: *fudge, cage*)

A Little Challenge

Prompt students to think of other Never or Always statements. They will find this difficult!

Most of the time:

The largest category of statements for students to develop or consider is based on "Most of the time . . ." Here are a few samples:

- Most of the time the /kw/ sound is spelled *qu* (as in *quit*; exceptions: *Kwanza*, *choir*).
- Most of the time, names of occupations end in *-er* or *-or* (as in *teacher* and *doctor*).
- Most of the time, after a short vowel, put *t* before *ch* (as in *ketchup*, *pitch*, *crutch*, and *dispatch*).

The whole idea of this work is so that students will be in a frame of inquiry based on noticing, wondering, and discovering.

Developing word detectives

Not long ago I was in a Grade 5 class where a teacher had generated interest in words throughout the year. I asked the students to share with me some of their wonderings about words. Here are a few of their thoughts.

> I wonder why *phone* starts with *ph*.
> I wonder why Canada and the United States have different spellings for the same words.
> I wonder why we have capital letters.
> I wonder why two letters make one sound, like *sh* or *ph*.
> I wonder why we have *y* sometimes as a vowel.

Students like these are paying attention to words, noticing their structure, and constantly adding insights. For example, they might notice that question words begin with *wh*: When? Where? Why? What? Which? Who? They might discover that certain words have no other words that rhyme with them — the four most common being *orange*, *silver*, *purple*, and *month*. Three are colors, which is interesting. Other words that lack a rhyme could be a subject for inquiry, or you may just want students to try to find out the four common ones.

Remember that, for students, the power is in the learning, not in being told. We can set students up for inquiry and investigation, but they need to do it themselves, and then, with the enthusiasm of word detectives who have found "gold," they can share their discoveries.

The only exceptions to the *tch* pattern I have found are the single syllable words *much*, *rich*, *such*, and *which*; and the multi-syllable words *ostrich*, *duchess*, *sandwich*, *attach*, and *bachelor*.

A Frame of Inquiry
I noticed that . . .
I wonder . . .
I discovered that most of the time . . .

7

Finding the Right Words

Check the Appendix for a student line master related to this color activity.

When students are engaged in writing, they often have to search for the right words to express what they want to say. Knowledge of literary devices, particularly simile and metaphor, often proves helpful.

When I was teaching Grade 5 and trying to engage students in metaphor, I found that the students were so much more comfortable with simile. They could create phrases like "as slow as a turtle" and "as angry as a hornet" with great ease. They could say someone was strong like a lion or able to fight like a tiger, but they found metaphor to be more complex. So I decided to play orally with colors and have them experiment with "Green is . . ., Blue is . . ., Purple is . . .," and this approach seemed to make it easier for them. They came up with phrases like *"Red is a fire-engine, speeding to the rescue."* Then one student wrote, *"Blue is the music of stars in space"* and I thought, that's it! If I introduce the senses in this work, the students will produce better writing. And they did. One student wrote, *"Brown is the sound of pine cones bursting."* My favorite response was created by a student for whom metaphor opened a new phase of writing. He wrote, *"Grey is the sound of dolphins talking."* We had come a long way from the literal *"Green is a leaf"*!

Going Beyond Literal Interpretation

To involve students of all ages in writing that uses metaphors or in learning to identify metaphors, you need to read aloud to them. Poetry is often better read aloud because students can practise visualization as a comprehension strategy. They can engage in critical thinking by trying to work out what the figurative language means. Doing so is worthwhile when you consider that the poorest scores on standardized assessments are often student responses to the poetry section in the Language booklet. It is not so much that the students are unable to read the poem but that they can't understand the language when it goes beyond literal interpretation.

Benefits associated with building knowledge of language

It needn't be this way. I visited a Grade 3 class where the teacher had done extensive work on looking at the author's message and having children interpret what the author was saying. She had read aloud the picture book *The Tower* by Richard Paul Evans, where a prince tries to build a high tower to show everyone how great he is and learns, instead, that is not how people achieve greatness. So I asked a student who was discussing with her group what the author's message was. Her reply: "That being great is not looking down on someone; being great is lifting someone up."

I found her answer magical. This student had not tested as gifted, and she attended a large multi-ethnic, multilingual school. How had she given such a thoughtful response? She and her classmates had a teacher who cared about teaching language, who constantly built word knowledge, who read aloud to the class daily, and who gave the students opportunities to write for a variety of purposes. The teacher also provided multiple opportunities to look for patterns in words, so that they were comfortable predicting how to spell a new word and able to use their current word knowledge to help them to edit. I left that classroom feeling so grateful that I had met another fine teacher.

I hope this example will encourage you to take your students past the literal and into a deep, constant search for the right words.

Exploring Metaphors

Metaphors are fascinating, so much so that I now keep a personal notebook where I collect them and recommend this "word therapy" to teachers as an excellent activity. As far as the classroom goes, instead of providing students with a definition of metaphor, you might have them examine these metaphors related to weather. You could highlight or underline the word acting as a metaphor to see whether they can figure it out.

> This homework is a <u>breeze</u>.
> She was so sad that her thinking was <u>clouded</u>.
> Her words hit him with the <u>force of hail</u>.
> His expression was <u>thunderous</u>.
> She faced a <u>storm</u> of criticism.
> His memory has been <u>foggy</u>.
> You'll be <u>blown away</u> when I share this story.

Idioms, which are discussed in Chapter 5, are a good precursor to metaphor, as they move students away from being literal into more expressive language. They take students from literal meaning to critical thinking when they work out what the figurative language means.

Students should be able to work out that weather terms are used to make the language more descriptive and interesting.

From these observations of metaphors, it is not much of a jump to come up with a definition such as this: the use of something unrelated to compare to something real to create more subtle meaning. *Homework* and *breeze* are unconnected, but when the author writes that homework is a breeze, she is trying to explain that the homework is as easy to complete as it is for a gentle breeze to blow softly by.

Students in Grades 4, 5, and 6 can hear more metaphors, try to understand them, and collect them from their own reading. Reading aloud text with examples would be beneficial for them. Here are a few famous examples from "The Highwayman," a poem by Alfred Noyes:

> The wind was a **torrent** of darkness among the gusty trees,
> The moon was a ghostly **galleon** tossed upon cloudy seas,
> The road was a **ribbon** of moonlight over the purple moor, . . .

The important connection is that students try to use metaphors in their writing, particularly when writing poetry.

Thinking about and collecting metaphors

Metaphors will give students ideas for writing, and they can collect them from many places. Students may be able to look at TV or magazine ads for metaphors. For example, United Airlines has a slogan, "Life is a journey — travel it well." Students can even create them in the context of their dreams. An old friend told me of her granddaughter sharing with her that she had had such a wonderful dream the previous night that she wanted to put a bookmark in it to keep her place. She said, "I put a bookmark in my dream." What a great line for the beginning of a poem! The idea is always to link back to writing and vocabulary building.

Metaphors are by no means limited to poetry. English surgeon John Lister used the metaphor "invisible assassins" to describe airborne germs. What is worth noting is that we *fight* infection. In the United States, the metaphor "fiscal cliff" has been coined and readily adopted to describe a dire financial crisis.

It is not so important that students know what metaphors are but that they use them in their writing. Here, some Grade 5 students are beginning to play with metaphors about weather, animals, and food:

> "Snow is a soft white marshmallow that falls on your tongue."
> "The tornado is a bey blade rolling on thunder."
> "Thunder is stomping elephants."
> "The storm was a fighter jet sweeping across the sky."
> "A rhino is thunder when it attacks its prey."
> "I am a cheetah running in the fields."
> "You are a snail crawling on the sidewalk."
> "Chocolate is a joyful piece of heaven, wrapped in a sparkling wrapper."

As students add to their vocabulary and images by exploring metaphor, they also need to understand the language of poetry, so that they can infer meaning when it is subtle and nuanced. A straightforward example would be unlocking meaning in StarField's poem "Joy," about winter appearing to last forever, then a green shoot appearing. The green leaf is a messenger announcing the arrival of spring. I read this poem, which can be found at silviahartmann.com/metaphor-poem.php, to students and then asked them to innovate on the structure. Students whom I worked with wrote their own metaphors, playing with this idea of contrasting seasons. Two examples:

> "Just when you thought
> that fall would never end,
> you saw,
> amidst the colourful leaves,
> a little bit of white
> the first snowflake to touch
> the voice of winter."

> "Just when you thought
> that summer will never end,
> you saw:
> a yellow-orange maple leaf,
> beautiful colours among the trees,
> the blowing winds yelling
> Fall is coming,
> Fall is coming."

The use of StarField's poem highlights the importance of mentor texts to give students ideas to integrate what they are learning about metaphor into their own poetry. Building schema of poetic images and their meanings is very important, as students tend to seek literal meaning if not exposed to multiple literary devices — the easiest one of all being alliteration.

Other Literary Devices

Other devices used in writing are alliteration, hyperbole, and personification, and these are discussed below. The purpose of all literary devices is to improve the phrase being written or to improve expression in the author's writing: to make the text more engaging to the reader.

Alliteration: As early as Grade 1, students are fascinated by phrases such as "wiggly, wriggly, worms," and "slithery snakes." Students enjoy this wordplay and later begin to create their own alliterative phrases in poetry and use descriptive devices in narrative.

Writers from Mother Goose to Edgar Allan Poe use alliteration. In "Three Grey Geese," the rhyme begins "Three grey geese in a green field grazing." In "The Raven," Edgar Allan Poe wrote, "While I nodded, nearly napping . . ." and "while I pondered, weak and weary." Students may want to search for alliteration in poetry and stories — Dr. Seuss would be one choice of author who would not disappoint.

Often, alliteration will help students to provide descriptions with more flair, although as with all devices, it can be overdone!

Hyperbole: Hyperbole is a literary device that students hear and use all the time — they just don't know its name! A parent might say: "Don't bother me! I'm doing a million things right now!" The parent wants to be left alone because she is busy, maybe doing two or three things at once. Students can use figures of speech orally for effect, especially if they are doing skits in Drama.

Typical student examples:

"I have been waiting for you forever!"
"I have tons of homework!"
"His car is about a hundred years old."
"I was so embarrassed, I almost died!"

Students don't need to know the term *hyperbole* so much as they need to know how to exaggerate for effect to add color to their oral presentations or skits, or perhaps in their writing.

Personification: Personification is a literary device whereby human qualities are granted to something not human. For example, consider this sentence: *The brakes on his car squealed.* People squeal, not brakes. Similarly, *the storm continued to brew* means that the storm was gaining power, not creating a stew in a stew pot. Other examples, *the words leapt off the page as she started to read*, *the trees moaned as I walked through the woods*, and *the avalanche raced down the mountainside*, all give human characteristics to non-human objects to make a point. In wordplay, students might enjoy matching certain emotions to certain objects for effect.

A Mischief of Mice, a Crash of Rhinos, a Scold of Jays

One way to help develop a lifelong fascination with words in students is to introduce them to the amazingly wide range of descriptors for groups of living creatures. Students may have heard of a "herd of cows," but there are many interesting descriptors they are unlikely to be familiar with. Terms such as the following are bound to tantalize and feed their poetic senses.

a kindle of kittens	a paddling of ducks
a flight of doves	a charm of finches
a drift of pigs	a knot of frogs
a shrewdness of apes	a herd, bloat, or crash of hippopotami
a swarm of butterflies	a scold of jays
a clutter or pounce of cats	a herd, mob, or troop of kangaroos
a chattering or clutch of chicks	a leap of leopards

There are many more names for groups of animals. Students can check the Internet or books for them. Some of the expressions might prompt writing. In fact, students may wish to create a picture book which illustrates and names a number of these groups. Or, they could create a PowerPoint or Prezi presentatation with animal photographs or sounds included.

Here are some picture book titles about these groups:

- *A Gaggle of Geese: The Collective Names of the Animal Kingdom* by Philippa-Ayls Browne (This book explains how the group name was derived.)
- *A Zeal of Zebras: An Alphabet of Collective Nouns* by Woop Studios
- *A Paddling of Ducks: Animals in Groups from A to Z* by Marjorie Parker
- *Have You Ever Seen a Smack of Jellyfish?: An Alphabet Book* by Sarah Asper-Smith

Adding Adjectives

As students build their word knowledge, it is important that they move from depending on the sounds in words to knowledge of the meanings of words, that they go from drawing on frequently used words to the use of less commonly used words, both in speaking and in writing. Therefore, when they are writing, they need to build their knowledge of and use of adjectives to help make their writing interesting. Students will use adjectives orally before they use them in writing. I walked into school with a Grade 1 student one day, who looked up at me and said, "I caught a snowflake on my tongue. It was delicious." Here was a young poet-in-waiting!

The line "It was a *dark* and *stormy* night . . . ," made famous by Charlie Brown, has been overused, but adjectives can help to give the reader more information about what the writer intended. In writer's craft, students use adjectives to describe for the reader what is happening in the text, whether it be fiction or non-fiction. To say that penguins swim in the *cold, icy* waters of the Antarctic helps the reader to understand that penguins live in a cold environment.

Students can collect phrases and begin lists as part of an effort to make their written work more interesting. They can learn about a few simple suffixes, or word endings, and add them to base words, thereby creating adjectives.

SUFFIXES		
-ous	*-ful*	*-less*
When you hear the sound /us/ at the end of a word, it is usually spelled *-ous*. It means "full of."	When you add *-ful* to a base word, it usually means "full of" but can also mean "able to" (e.g., harmful, helpful) or "as much as will fill" (e.g., spoonful, cupful).	When you want to describe something, you can add *-less* to a base word. This suffix means "lacking or without."
dangerous	care + ful = careful	careless
adventurous	frightful	homeless
famous	helpful	helpless
monstrous	cheerful	useless
poisonous	tearful	cloudless
mountainous	forgetful	cordless
humorous	respectful	endless

Students can expand their lists for adjectives by identifying basic words and adding synonyms as they find them in their reading and as they look for the best synonym to help them in their writing.

Check the Appendix for a student line master related to this adjective-finding activity.

Basic Word	Interesting Adjectives
big	large, huge, enormous, gigantic
little	small, tiny, miniature, compact
hot	bright, scorching, tropical
cold	cool, frosty, icy, glacial
loud	noisy, blaring, deafening, earsplitting
soft	comfortable, furry, pliable, velvety

Students need to collect synonyms for common words and then add to them as they find the words they like to use because, in certain contexts, some words work so much better than others. You can say that a pillow is as *soft* as a feather, but a chair tends to be *comfortable*. Collecting antonyms, or opposites, for example, strong/weak, good/bad, high/low, is also a good idea.

Circle activities to promote fluency of description

An activity to achieve fluency of description is to ask students to sit in a circle and then explain that the class is going to describe how they feel when it is cold. Begin by giving an example: "It was so cold that I thought I was going to turn into an icicle." Then, give each student a turn to say something beginning with "It was so cold that . . ." At first, they may be literal: "It was so cold that I put on extra layers of clothes." However, since this activity is short enough that you can do it often, you will find that they get better. Soon you will be hearing statements such as, "It was so cold that I no longer believed in global warming."

Options to this activity are many: It was so hot that . . . ; it was so dark that . . . ; it was so stormy that . . . ; it was so deep that . . . ; it was so scary that . . . ; it was so bright that . . .. Students can also change the beginning to "the night was so dark that . . .," and so on.

In this circle, you are building community with a common task and building language orally because everyone joins in. You are also strengthening students' confidence, as they are able to do an exercise like this on a regular basis. (If a student is unsure of what to say, he or she can pass, or repeat an earlier example, and there is always a sentence that can be repeated because the teacher goes first.)

The circle can be adapted to any activity, including simile making, whether students know the word *simile* or not: as deep as, as clear as, as wide as. As with all new activities, this focus is more difficult for Grade 3 students when they begin. At first, they will come up with phrases along these lines: as white as snow, as white as chalk; as clear as glass, as clear as air, as clear as water; as wide as the ocean, as wide as the earth; as deep as the bottom of the ocean, as deep as the bottom of a cliff. With practice, students become more proficient. After just two practice sessions, the same students who produced the answers above generated these more interesting responses:

> "It was so hot that I felt like I was on fire."
> "It was so hot that a thousand fans were not enough!"
> "It was so hot that I got dehydrated."
> "It was so hot that I almost melted."
> "It was so hot that I felt I was in a volcano full of lava."

Then,

> "It was so deep that I couldn't find rock bottom."
> "It was so deep that I couldn't see sunlight."
> "It was so deep that I couldn't see the surface."
> "It was so deep that I couldn't get out."
> "It was so deep that I could see dinosaur bones."

And finally,

> "It was so scary that I fainted."
> "It was so scary that I had nightmares."
> "It was so scary that I felt like cuddling my teddy bear."
> "It was so scary that I ran all the way home."
> "It was so scary that it took my breath away!"

A talking stick or an object to pass around the circle would help here, as it would focus attention on the current speaker.

What has been built here, over just a few lessons, is *descriptive confidence*, something that will increase with practice and variety, but the aspect of community is important, as students inspire one another to greater expression. This activity is enjoyable and low threat for students; they find it hard to wait their turn to participate.

Exploring Character Traits Through Adjectives

Students can identify the main character in a book fairly easily and describe this person to a peer or to the teachers. The word *trait*, however, gives some students, especially young ones, a problem if the word is rarely used. If it is repeated often, though, they become familiar with the idea of a character trait being quite different from a character in a story. They come to recognize it as a way to describe the character.

In another Grade 3 classroom I visited, a teacher was building vocabulary by listing character traits. She started by listing two or three words, and then built the list throughout the year from the characters that the students encountered in their reading. Because they had met all of these words in context, the students were comfortable using the words on this list, both to talk about character traits and to write about them.

This chart reflects the recopied, neat version that students could continue to read easily and use regularly. The four-column chart, with positive characteristics in the left column, negative characteristics in the next column, and a mix of positive and negative descriptors in the last two columns, was built with students over many weeks.

caring	mean	courageous	fighter
helpful	bossy	serious	determined
respectful	rude	funny	energetic
friendly	disrespectful	timid	cheerful
unselfish	selfish	shy	calm
loving	disagreeable	bold	mannerly
generous	lazy	daring	adventurous
considerate	carefree	dainty	mischievous
honest	demanding	fun-loving	intelligent
thoughtful	stubborn	successful	independent
loyal	conceited	dreamer	humble
cooperative		happy	self-confident
hard-working		leader	inventive
patriotic		messy	imaginative
responsible		neat	demanding
polite		quiet	naïve
		curious	creative
		witty	

The date February 7, 2012, was the 200th anniversary of the birth of Charles Dickens. Dickens is still known for the strong characters he created — Oliver Twist, Ebenezer Scrooge, to name two. Many people who have never even read Dickens's books know his characters! He built memorable ones.

What I found interesting about visiting this classroom was the fluency with which these students, most of whom were English Language Learners, were able to talk about characters expressively. They integrated the words from the list into their speaking vocabulary and then transferred this to their writing.

Note that this chart (or one like it) could also be used to look at spelling patterns in adjectives by, for example, listing words with the suffix *-ous* and adding to the list; finding words with the suffix *-ful* and adding to the list, and so on.

Considering Adverbs Too

When students describe characters in their writing, they may use adjectives to add interest to nouns, but they can also use adverbs to add interest to their writing. Only a few rules relate to the spelling of adverbs. As the list below shows, the usual way to make an adverb from an adjective is to add *-ly*.

quick	quick**ly**	rude	rude**ly**
patient	patient**ly**	brave	brave**ly**
slow	slow**ly**	neat	neat**ly**

warm	warm**ly**	anxious	anxious**ly**
beautiful	beautiful**ly**	bad	bad**ly**
loud	loud**ly**	curious	curious**ly**
nice	nice**ly**		

Students may wish to develop lists to check whether most adverbs are really formed this way. (They are.)

In a slight variation, if an adjective ends in -*y*, the adverb is usually formed by changing *y* to *i* and adding -*ly*. Examples:

happy, happily; heavy, heavily; lazy, lazily; lucky, luckily

There are a few exceptions, but they are confined to words of one syllable: *shy, shyly; coy, coyly; wry, wryly*.

If an adjective ends in -*ic*, the adverb is usually formed by adding -*ally*. Examples:

dramatic, dramatically; drastic, drastically;
tragic, tragically; automatic, automatically

Exception: *public, publicly*.

If an adjective ends in -*ble*, the adverb is created by changing the ending to -*bly*.

responsible, responsibly; capable, capably; comfortable, comfortably;
probable, probably; respectable, respectably; predictable, predictably

This information is more for teacher use when giving descriptive feedback. When a child has spelled an adverb wrongly, perhaps writing "He put down his pen *angryly*," you can respond that the common way to create an adverb is to do exactly what the child did — add -*ly* to the root word; in this case, though, the adjective would have ended in -*y*, so when an adjective ending in -*y* is changed into an adverb, the -*y* is changed to *i* to produce *angrily*. You can then give the student some examples, such as *happy, happily* and *lazy, lazily*.

Similarly, if a child writes "*probabley*," you can tell the student that adverbs end in -*bly*, not "-bley" and show examples of adjectives changing to adverbs. You may also do a mini-lesson on adverbs for students who are having problems spelling them. They would see this as relevant just-in-time word knowledge, as opposed to disconnected information, not relevant to their writing.

Using analogies to support learning about adverbs

Creating questions around analogies to change adjectives to adverbs is an activity for practice.

- *Quick* is to *quickly*, as *safe* is to _____.
- *Loud* is to *loudly*, as _____ is to *slowly*.
- _____ is to *rudely*, as *fair* is to *fairly*.

These are regular adverbs, which follow the rule to add -*ly*. You could expand the activity to include other adverbial changes, too, for example, changing -*y* to *i* and adding -*ly*.

Students should also keep a list of adverbs they use in their writing. Prompt them to build their vocabulary by adding interesting adverbs from their reading.

A Word of Caution

Students have a tendency to overuse what they have just learned: for example, Grade 1 students learn about periods and then insert them at the end of every word. Eventually, though, they work out where the periods go. Similarly, there is a danger that students will overuse adjectives and adverbs in their writing. Students need to learn that if they are to communicate effectively, they will have to add adjectives and adverbs judiciously.

The Fun Side of Collecting Words

Students who play with words, pay attention to the makeup of words, and engage with words tend to become good spellers — they are constantly noticing and analyzing word formation. They can engage in wordplay, as in punning, while collecting words and phrases. From an early age, children enjoy knock, knock jokes, which are often built around puns. Two simple examples:

Knock, knock.	Knock, knock.
Who's there?	Who's there?
Amos.	Anna.
Amos who?	Anna who?
A mosquito.	An other mosquito.

Students of all ages can quote or recall knock, knock jokes. Even students who are not inclined to finish reading a regular novel often finish many books of jokes, such as these ones:

- *National Geographic Kids Just Joking: 300 Hilarious Jokes, Tricky Tongue Twisters and Ridiculous Riddles* by National Geographic Kids
- *101 Hockey Jokes* by Kara Woodburn
- *The World's Greatest Knock-Knock Jokes for Kids* by Bob Phillips

Playing with multiple word meanings

Exposing students to puns is a way for them to play with multiple word meanings. For example, consider these simple puns (which come from www.buzzle.com/articles/puns-for-kids.html):

What do you call a sleeping bull? A bulldozer.
Why are the fish smart? Because they live in schools.

If students decide to create "punny" jokes, they may find the following books helpful:

- *Mr. Putney's Quacking Dog* by Jon Agee
- *Rhyme and Punishment: Adventures in Wordplay* by Brian P. Cleary
- *Punny Places: Jokes to Make You Happy* by June Swanson

Defining words in a punny way

One way for students to learn about defining words is to approach them in a punny way. A number of years ago, I decided to create a book of wordplays with my Grade 5 class. We had already shared numerous books on puns and engaged in wordplay. We had also worked on multiple words with literal definitions. I wanted the element of play. We used the word *ant*.

My class and I began with this definition of *ant* to set a playful tone:

ant: a small, hard-working insect that always finds time to go on picnics.

Students worked in pairs to define several other words and then we put all the ideas together. Some words had *ant* at the beginning, some used the prefix *anti-*, and some had *ant* at the end of the word, where it means a person who or the thing which. We found enough material with this ending to develop a lengthy book. Some *ant* examples:

> **antler:** the branched deciduous horn of any member of the ant family. [You can see that this student modeled his definition on a dictionary definition.]

> **anteater:** a picnic-raiding ant who is truly gluttonous, and whose motto is "If at first you aren't full, eat, eat, eat again!"

> **antorney:** a distinguished legal ant [This word was created by the students; it is not a misspelling.)

> **antique:** an ancient ant, who likes to sleep on the shelf in a store with other valuable artifacts

> **dominant:** the principal ant in the colony, who antagonizes all smaller ants

> **elephant:** the largest members of the ant colony

> **jubilant:** partying ants, who are constantly joyful

The book of definitions was read and reread. It caused laughter and learning because students were now aware of the ending *-ant* and developed an interest in words with that ending. They even created a serious sequel with the correct definitions of the featured words. By this time, students were sharing the "Ant" book throughout the school, and they wanted to ensure that no one would be confused.

As part of a community of learners who constantly wondered about words, these students generated and explored the question "Do more words end in *-ant* or *-ent*?" They noticed that they did not always know which ending to use. In this instance, brainstormed lists helped them.

Students began to build a list, short at first, and then every time they came across another word, they added it. They would come up to me on yard duty, saying, "I have another word for the list — *continent*!" If we were lining up for recess, they would offer to add a word to the list. Their list was much longer than the one shown below.

I was amazed at how much wordplay and skill had tied together naturally, but then I reflected that the question had come from the children and that I had first involved them in wordplay and investigations. I recommend that students engaged in a similar exploration keep a T-chart and fit words they use into the correct column. In English, more words end in *-ent* than *-ant*, but the list of words students generate may show otherwise, and that is all right.

-ant endings	*-ent* endings
brilliant	confident
consonant	congruent
distant	continent
dominant	current
elephant	continent
hesitant	different
important	equivalent
instant	evident
relevant	excellent
tolerant	impatient
	independent
	intelligent
	present
	recent
	resident
	silent
	urgent

Building word knowledge can be quite fascinating, and many students will independently complete investigations. Encourage them to share their discoveries with others and to keep making inquiries.

Sample Checklists for Revising and Editing

So, what do students need to look for as a result of the information in this chapter? The following sample checklist with questions could be used if appropriate for the text form students have chosen.

When I revise my writing, I will consider the following:	Check
Was it useful to use metaphor in this piece of writing?	
Was it useful to compare by using a simile in this piece? (as _____ as a _____)	
Did I improve my descriptions by using adjectives? Example: When I shook his *icy* hand, I wondered if the *cold, northern* climate had pierced his bones.	
Did I describe more fully by the use of adverbs? Example: He was *badly* injured in the car crash.	

Here is another sample checklist, which students may use all or part of, as they revise their own writing. The teacher is trying to encourage self-sufficiency here.

When I revise my writing, I will consider the following:	Check
Did I add to my list of synonyms for common words?	
Have I added to my list of character traits?	
Have I added to my collection of puns, which I may be able to use as wordplay in my writing?	
Have I added to my list of *-ant/-ent* words, so that I can use them when I edit my work?	

As always, these revision checklists would be adapted to the material you are teaching; however, there needs to be a direct link and application to students' writing, revising, and editing. As a result, the list could have few or many items. I would actively encourage students to keep a list of character traits from Grade 3 onward. They will gain many descriptors for the multitude of characters they encounter — human, android, or animal.

Editing for spelling always follows revision, because the piece of writing has to be close to completion before spelling seriously begins to matter. At that point, many spelling errors would be like "loud background noise" interfering with the reader's focus. So, an editing checklist could involve a few or several of the following:

I can edit by . . .	Check
checking the spelling of metaphors I have used in my writing	
checking the spelling of character trait terms I used from my list	
checking the spelling of character trait terms I am adding to my list	
checking the spelling of adjectives I have used	
checking the spelling of synonyms I am using or listing	
checking the spelling of words ending in *-ant* and *-ent*	
checking the spelling of words ending in *-ance* and *-ence*	

However, this list would be adapted to individual or group needs so may look more like this or the sample below it.

I can edit by . . .	Check
checking the spelling of character trait terms I used from my list	
checking the spelling of synonyms I am using or listing	
checking the spelling of words ending in *-ant* and *-ent*	

I can edit by . . .	Check
checking the spelling of metaphors I have used in my writing and adding them to my collection of metaphors	
checking the spelling of adjectives I have used and adding them to my list of adjectives	
checking the spelling of adverbs I have used and adding them to my list of adverbs	

Application is what counts, so the fact that students have growing word and language knowledge matters only when they can apply it directly to their writing. Slowly but surely, students will become word users who edit, make inquiries, and bring more and more information to the words they write.

8

Writing Is Always the Context

A *mentor text* is a text used as a model for student writing. The purpose and structure of the mentor text is carefully chosen according to purpose and then clearly explained by the teacher. The teacher may use a book, a poem, a descriptive paragraph, or a piece of student writing as a mentor text.

Writing is not always easy, and we know that fluency increases the ability to write. So we need to give students opportunities to write in a variety of ways and in a variety of contexts so that their fluency increases. Many student writers follow the process of generating ideas, finding a purpose for their writing, making decisions to choose relevant ideas and discard others, organizing what is left, reviewing the purpose for the piece, composing, finding their voice in the piece, revising, and finally proofreading and editing their work. Students also need to be connected over and over again to mentor texts, so that they will have numerous fine models to draw from.

As we near the end of this book, it is appropriate for me to reinforce its emphasis: to enable students to proofread and edit their work at the last stage of the writing process. If student writers have nothing to say, any ability to spell correctly seems redundant.

Generating Ideas Together — The Importance of Talk

Before determining purpose for their writing, students usually generate ideas about what to say. When *generating ideas* for writing, talk is essential. When asked to recount a personal experience, for example, students probably find it helpful to orally share an experience first with a partner and then with someone else. As students explain an idea or experience out loud to someone else, their ideas achieve greater clarity. A good practice is for each partner to make one positive comment and then ask one clarifying question.

This type of sharing can be continued with students taking opposite points of view, as in the examples below.

Viewpoint #1	Viewpoint #2
People should be allowed to have pets.	People should NOT be allowed to have pets.
Raccoons and squirrels are intruders in our backyards.	Raccoons and squirrels were here before these homes were built, so we are the intruders.
Recycling is enough!	We need to reduce and reuse as well as recycle.
Healthy food is delicious.	Junk food tastes better!

Viewpoint #1	Viewpoint #2
Electric cars, or some even newer technology, will be the future.	Hybrid cars are the future.
Endangered animals are just a part of the process of nature.	We are responsible for helping to save endangered animals.

Students can decide as a class which two topics to focus on, then pick one of the topics and generate three ideas in support of their point of view. They then need to meet first with one and then with a second student who has the same topic and point of view. Students can add to their list of reasons to support this point of view. They then meet with two students who hold the opposite point of view and listen to their reasons. They need to choose at least two of these arguments and try to refute them, making notes as they think about the issue. Both sides now have the basis of a simple argument. In this case, the *purpose* of their writing would be to persuade.

If students decide to adopt the opposite point of view after they have begun talking to others, they may do so. The voice in their writing would then be stronger. Just as talking, thinking, and writing have been a part of these activities, they need to be very much a part of the writing process.

Establishing Purpose

Purpose is the key factor in all writing, and in part because of this, students may need to be reminded of the variety of purposes associated with writing. All authors want to connect with their audience, and purpose determines how they will do this. As for teachers, they typically want their student writers to communicate clearly, think critically, and reflect on what they write.

Mainly through working with teachers and students, I have come to identify the following as key purposes for writing:

- to persuade or convince; to justify an opinion, or point of view, with relevant evidence
- to instruct (through procedure)
- to inform and report (by sharing facts, as in a blog or a written report)
- to inspire and help the reader connect to a big idea
- to present an issue and make a call to social action
- to narrate (in fiction and non-fiction)
- to describe
- to summarize
- to respond to something read
- to record or recount personal or in-role experiences on a regular basis (e.g., in a log, diary, or online journal)
- to entertain

This list is not exhaustive. Indeed, you can likely add to it. Some of these purposes may be combined: for example, students can write a descriptive report or explain the issue on which they are expressing a point of view before they justify their stance.

One goal for teachers is to encourage student writers to think critically and develop informed opinions so that the link between reading and writing becomes more obvious. When students become connected to social action, they are engaged rather than passive, and so will write letters to companies and begin to understand the political process of change in a democracy. They will seek to inspire others by helping the reader to connect to a big idea, such as environmental stewardship or global citizenship. Students may see that writers often need to do some research before they write, so that they are well informed on their subject and can offer relevant evidence in support of their point of view.

So, how do authors achieve their purpose?

Authors achieve their purpose in a variety of ways. They do it by choosing their words carefully. They do it by connecting with the reader through their voice and through their experience. They do it by clarifying ideas through explanations, by sharing different points of view, and by helping the reader to connect to a wider range of ideas. They do it by justifying their point of view through supporting evidence. They do it by inspiring the reader through careful use of metaphors and by highlighting how to play a part in creating meaningful change. They also do it by writing so powerfully that they can change opinions, biases, and perspectives.

These are only some of the ways that authors achieve their purpose, but these ideas serve to demonstrate the complexity of writing and the importance of knowing the author's purpose. Depending on the reason for writing, purpose may come first, but more often, the writing process begins by generating ideas. There is no wrong way to begin, just what works for the teacher and the students on each piece. Discussing the process could be very profitable.

To summarize, then, writers may go through the following process . . .

- generating ideas
- deciding on purpose
- choosing and discarding ideas as they start to focus
- organizing the ideas that are left (researching, if necessary)
- revisiting purpose
- composing
- bringing voice to the writing to connect with the reader
- revising
- proofreading and editing work

If spelling interferes with the ability to reread work, as the author is revising, it needs to be addressed; otherwise, it does not become important until the revisions are complete and the student is proofreading the work for errors.

When It's Time to Address Spelling

Many people have trouble finding every error in their work, so here are some guiding questions to help students as they proofread:

- Does every syllable have a vowel or *y*? Check long words carefully.

- Are your vowel combinations correct? (Examples: *ai, ay, a_e; ea, ee; ie, i_e; oi, oo, o _e; ui* (guide), *u_e*.) Circle those you are unsure of.
- Do your endings look right? (Examples: walk, walk**ed**; carry, carr**ied**)
- Did you make plurals correctly? (Examples: dog, dog**s**; box, box**es**, puppy, pupp**ies**)
- Did you check for silent letters? (Examples: **k**nob, **w**rong, cas**t**le)
- Have you looked for perhaps two or three words that give you trouble?

Students may begin by checking their work for one of these at a time; then, as they become more aware of words and of the words they misspell, they should be able to create questions for self-editing. To create questions for editing, they will need to build self-awareness and to identify problem spelling in their final drafts.

Possible questions students could ask themselves are these:

> Do I seem to have more trouble with endings? Which endings? Past tenses of vowels? Plurals? Suffixes?
>
> Are there common words that I constantly misspell? (Examples: *was, friend, beautiful*)
>
> Can I tell if a word looks right or not, when I reread my written work?
>
> Do I find it easier to check a friend's work for errors than my own? (Peer editing would be the answer here.)
>
> When there are mini-lessons in spelling, do I make a note and apply this information when I write?

Before students can create their own questions and as they develop self-awareness, they will need much practice working with teacher-created questions related to the large body of word knowledge they are constantly building and regularly applying directly to their writing.

Proofreading for spelling

The distinction I make between proofreading and editing is that proofreading is finding the errors, and editing is fixing them.

When they begin to proofread, students often need a peer or the teacher to help them. They could search for five common mistakes that the teacher and students have identified the class as making (or that they have identified themselves as making). They could check their writing for one or two words at a time — a very doable approach that puts them in control. Students also need to devise and use viable editing checklists from the numerous sample lists.

Application — the key factor

Just as important as proofreading is building word consciousness or, as Richard Gentry puts it, "spelling consciousness," so that students

- investigate words constantly and ask questions about them
- think about the construction of words
- seek to match new words to patterns
- note words carefully in their personal dictionaries, Word Work notebooks, Writer's Craft notebooks, or books of spelling lists, if they don't seem to fit a pattern

If students have poor visual memories, it is harder for them to proofread. In this case, they need lots of practice considering whether words look right. You may want to have them do the exercise on pages 35 and 36.

- become aware of silent letters and keep lists of the ones they use
- know how to form plurals, adjectives, and adverbs
- know how prefixes and suffixes work

This list would get lengthier as students learn more.

In previous times, students could achieve perfect scores on spelling tests, but not often apply this knowledge to their writing; therefore, as teachers, we need to keep the balance between building word knowledge and applying it to writing. We also need to be prepared to change the bias we have on spelling to what we do in mathematics. If a student has two errors out of 100 in a quiz in mathematics, we say that the student has achieved 98 percent. If a student has two errors in spelling in a piece of writing, we say that the student has made two mistakes. What is positive is that we now view mathematics as problem solving with numbers — it is time to view spelling as problem solving with words. So, if a student wrote "I went to the movies with my freinds," we would give feedback like this: "All the letters are there, but what can you tell me about the vowels?" If the student is able to self-correct, you would be encouraging, but if the student finds your comment confusing, it is time to review a commonly misspelled high-frequency word. As you encourage your writers who are learning to spell, you will want them to become lovers and investigators of words, who develop schema to proofread and edit.

Digital Literacy and Students Making Use of Technology

As teachers, we may think of writing as involving pen and paper, but students of the 21st century have multiple digital tools at their fingertips, and it is important for us to recognize and encourage the use of these tools in the modern classroom.

I had the privilege of working for three months as an interim vice-principal in Treeline Public School, in Ontario's Peel District School Board, which is on the cutting edge of technology. Treeline, a school with solar panels on the roof to create energy, is completely wireless. It is a Junior Kindergarten to Grade 8 school with about 850 students. Students and teachers are highly engaged in what they do.

Because talk precedes writing, particularly in lower grades, here is a way to use descriptive feedback to encourage self-monitoring: flip video cameras. Grade 1 teachers share their oral language assessment rubric with students and ask them to create a story to tell or a short experience to share. The students practise this, and then the teachers use the flip cameras to take video clips of their oral performances. These clips are shared individually with children; then, descriptive feedback — a key strategy for improvement in oral work, writing, and spelling — in the form of two stars and a wish is given. Two stars means two positive attributes they have shown; a wish might tell them, for example, that it is important to make eye contact with the audience. The students celebrate what they did well and almost always self-correct the next time.

These same Grade 1 students use netbooks to write so when they reach higher grades, they will be able to research work with one or more partners on a platform like PREZI.

A *flip camera* is a small, tapeless video camera, which records digitally. It uses flash memory to record up to two hours of video. Flip cameras are used from Kindergarten through to Grade 8, but as the students get older, they use the cameras rather than the teachers.

Giving feedback through frameworks like Prezi

The Grade 5 students told me that one of their Prezis on ancient civilizations had 108 slides. For this project, they usually worked in pairs, but the platform would allow up to 10 people to sign in and work together at the same time.

Integrating writing into a subject such as Social Studies, where students use literacy skills to research, write, and edit, can be enhanced by working on a digital framework, such as Prezi.

I asked some Grade 5 students who had completed projects on ancient civilizations in pairs to talk to me about how they were able to do this project electronically. I began to take notes about what they were saying, and they indulged me, but they were much more comfortable when I listened to their suggestion to take out my iPhone to record their comments, so I would not miss anything (the recording was deleted the same day). Students told me that Prezi is digital cloud-based software that gives them something like a giant piece of Bristol board or a canvas, which they can animate and use to create a pathway of information. They can import and display information, pictures, and videos. They can create work on a virtual canvas. What differentiates this program from just a telephone line, a cable, or a wireless connection and a laptop in front of the writer is that through sharing an email address, students can contribute to the same large piece of work online at the same time. Each partner can see what the other is doing and give and receive feedback. This is truly a joint effort, where the student can be in class or at home and continue with the work, while creating a longer and longer pathway through the presentation.

If you have an Apple computer or iPad, I strongly recommend that you download the App, or, if you have a PC, go to the website at www.prezi.com. You can read all about Prezi and take the tutorial. The site may ask you to sign up by entering your email address and creating a password. Access is free. You may want to practise by loading a PowerPoint slide presentation into PREZI to see the difference it can make.

Prezi allows users to move anywhere on the large digital canvas so that they can zero in on information, videos, and photographs, all without the need to travel to someone's home to do their work as a group. From the point of view of spelling and editing, Prezi permits many eyes to be on the same piece of writing, and students can collaborate to proofread and edit. In the Grade 5 class I worked with, the enthusiasm to write was palpable.

The Grade 5 students I talked with were highly engaged, and when they shared their presentations with me, I was impressed by their depth and unique design elements as well as the vast amount of resources the students had drawn on. Every one of these students talked about their teacher, for whom they had the utmost respect, and commended her on the way she had encouraged them to engage in this complex project, even in the face of technical difficulties initially beyond their control. Not one of them would have preferred to hand in a booklet, and all students told me that they had worked harder and longer on this project than they would have if it had been in paper format. What also impressed me was the care they had taken to write and then proofread and edit on such a large project, and the high level of accuracy they had achieved through multiple proofreaders and peer editors, who looked at the text again and again.

The Prezi website will also provide access to sample presentations under "Prezis we like." If you view a few of them, you will likely be impressed by the possibilities of this program to engage your students.

Because Prezi is a collaborative, interactive platform, students have access to one another's work and can give feedback at any stage of the process. By Grade 6, students are much more familiar with many of the Web 2.0 tools and are able to collaborate easily to write, even creating a plan to share before they begin to write.

The following outline and short descriptive piece were developed on a Crocodoc platform. After the Grade 6 student drafted his plan online, he received feedback from peers, which is reflected in his final plan, below:

> *The Worst Day of My Life*
> Intro: How it started (wake up)
> Fell down the stairs

```
               Forgot to do homework
               Missed the bus
     Middle:   Throughout the day (at school, after school)
               Bad test marks
               Lots of homework
               Computer broke down so couldn't go on it
               Had no dinner
     End:      At home
               Going to sleep
               Hope for a better day
```

Because of descriptive feedback from peers, the student was able to write this descriptive paragraph. Using the outline he had revised and developed, he wrote this final version of his paragraph online:

As soon as I woke up, I knew this was going to be my worst day ever. When I was sleepily trudging downstairs, I fell and landed with a thud. "OW!" I yelled, as I rubbed my sore head. With a throbbing head, I still remembered one thing: I didn't do my homework again! The teacher would *be* furious at me. With terror, I slowly turned around to face the clock. The time was 8:45, and the bus would be in front of the driveway any minute! Quickly, I grabbed what I thought was everything and ran to the door. "Too late," I thought to myself, as the bus passed by me. Fast as a cheetah, I ran with all my power to the school, hoping I could make it before I was late for class. Once again, I was too late and too slow, as I had to regretfully hand in my millionth late slip. Class wasn't better either, as when I apprehensively informed the teacher I forgot my homework at home, I was given even more homework! Last week's test was horrible, as I got a D-. When school was finally over, I ran straight back home and looked up the new homework on my computer. Unfortunately, when I arrived home, the computer was broken, as it fell off its stand. Now what was I going to do? Tell Ms. Thing that I didn't do my homework again? Disregarding that fact, I thought of food, and in my fridge, there was no food! So I went to bed hungry, depressed, and upset. After the torment I had been through that day, all I could think of was about the next day and if it would be better.

So, the student drafted a plan to write, received feedback on his plan, created a better plan, and wrote a better paragraph. He carefully proofread and edited his work.

Crocodoc is a good program to use for a smaller project. In this instance, where the student had omitted the word *be* from his final draft, other students could draw arrows and point out the omission.

Prezi is a better platform than Crocodoc for co-creating work. In a final Prezi done in June 2012, these Grade 6 students responded to the question "How can technology tools help you to engage in a social network, research collaboratively, and develop online products/activities to help display your understanding?" Since they were truly familiar with many Web 2.0 tools, the students began by identifying the tools and resources they had used that school year. These included Twiddla, MSN, Prezi, Brainpop, Crocodoc, Engrade, Edmodo, Weebly, YouTube, National Film Board (sometimes), Skype, online Jeopardy game,

Bitstrips, Educreations, Grolier (sometimes), Encyclopedia Britannica Online (sometimes), Khan Academy, Learn 360, Explore Learning, and AVS Video Editor (sometimes).

Students had explored how these tools helped them to engage in a social network as they collaborated to learn together.

Social networking tools useful for writing and editing

The following section is comprised of comments by various Grade 6 students exposed to social networking tools in the classroom.

> **MSN:** "Honestly, MSN was one of the most helpful tools when it came to communicating with my peers. I was able to co-ordinate work, share work, and help lead with group conversations. I could have been at home and still known exactly what to do, when to do it, and what to do with the help of MSN. With MSN, I didn't have to be in my classroom to create work. It was that easy."
>
> **Crocodoc:** "Crocodoc helps me with my work a lot because, say, if I were on a vacation far away, and had an assignment, where we were at the stage of editing one another's work, I can edit from wherever I am, and my group can edit my work, and look at all the edits I made. Personally, Crocodoc is the most straightforward and easy to use editing tool."
>
> **Twiddla:** "I found Twiddla very helpful, for example, if we have to work in a group and we are not able to meet up, there is a neat feature on Twiddla that lets you voice call. So whoever is on chat in your group could hear what you are saying. So it's kind of like talking on the phone, but you're working at the same time."
>
> **Edmodo:** "Edmodo is a very helpful tool when it comes to sharing ideas, asking your peers to help and communicating with your teacher. Even your parents can communicate with your teacher with a parent account. Edmodo also helps keep all of your work organized with the Edmodo library. Using Edmodo as my class site has helped me organize my work and it helps me keep track of everything I need to do with notifications listed on the side. This way I know everything I need to do."
>
> **Prezi:** "Prezi was a good way to collaborate and work with each other. It was a great use for an information base."
>
> **Engrade:** "Engrade was also a great tool. I used Engrade in order to communicate with my teacher. I could always receive help from wherever I was. I'm also able to easily share any information with him. Not only my teacher, but I can also contact my classmates. My parents also found this tool useful because they were up-to-date with what we were doing (thanks to the emailing feature) and were able to communicate with my teacher as well."

These are just some of the ways students were able to engage in social networking. They cited many other ways with equal enthusiasm.

Technology tools useful for collaborative research

Students collaborated online to consider how technology tools could help them do collaborative research.

YouTube: "When we go to YouTube and we are trying to research our topic, it helps us to visualize by watching videos. We were able to easily access visuals like pictures and videos about any topic. Most importantly we found the most recent information about certain topics: for example, NASA's thoughts about Mars."

Google: "It helped us, because by just typing in a statement specifically on your topic, we get many replies in return helping us with a great amount of research."

Learn 360: "Instead of just going to 6 different websites, we can just go to one and find all of our videos that we have been watching for the whole year. There are a variety of videos that explain different topics. It makes learning easier and more interesting."

Technology tools in the context of citizenship

Finally, students were asked a key question by their teacher: "Why is it imperative to address the importance of being a responsible citizen before allowing students to use any technology in the classroom?" Two collaborating students provided a thoughtful answer:

> The rights and responsibilities of Canadian Citizenship include: "Freedom of thought, belief, opinion and expression, including freedom of speech and of the press" while respecting the rights and freedoms of others. This needs to be addressed, as the same regard is to be exercised by students when they are online and communicating and interacting with others such as their peers, teachers, etc.

They concluded by citing this reference: http://www.cic.gc.ca/english/resources/publications/discover/section-04.asp.

The Grade 6 teacher who worked with these students had thoughtfully integrated technology into every aspect of their learning. As a result, the classroom was a vibrant community, where students used technology as easily as breathing. However, since he was aware that boundaries matter, the teacher had put in place a student protocol:

> *Protocol for using tools of technology:*
> 1. Use tool thoughtfully. (Begin with the end in mind — is this tool going to help me achieve success in an efficient way?)
> 2. Reflect on personal use frequently and use tool to help track/develop plans for success (Evernote, calendars, etc.).
> 3. Monitor and support peer use frequently because there are opportunities to learn and protect personal freedoms/privileges of use.
> — *Andrew Dobbie,* Grade 6 teacher

These students demonstrated to me on every visit that they were creative collaborators and thoughtful problem-solvers. Although technology enhanced their abilities, their success was a result of daily opportunities to think, collaborate, and solve problems in a variety of contexts, including some that involved words.

Peer Editing Online

So, if students could do all that I have outlined above in Grade 6, how could they extend this in Grade 7? Well, they could become more proficient at giving descriptive feedback to peers, embodying all the respect and thoughtful responses they had been taught. They could develop "All about my life" websites, and as one part of this work, write responses to books just read.

Having read and implemented the tenets of *The Book Whisperer: Awakening the Inner Reader in Every Child* by Donalyn Miller, the Grade 7 teachers at Treeline engaged the students in reading from a wide variety of genres. Students were encouraged to read books outside their favorite genre to expand their exposure to texts. They wrote responses to the books they read, and the Grade 7 teachers made suggestions on other books to read, on how to improve the reflection in their reading responses, and so on. Students' responses improved, and they were able to give feedback to their peers. They used technology to do this and had a closed Weebly platform for sharing work — the Weebly is password protected, and each class was closed to anyone outside. The teacher, of course, had access.

An example of effective online dialogue

The whole idea of proofreading and editing is, I believe, contained in the extended example presented below. The two students featured were online and in-class partners. They were expected to make reading responses on the books they were reading. Having a partner (or multiple partners) give advice on proofreading and editing was intended to enhance their work. There was thus a direct link to writing and a direct application to the work at hand. Through the online dialogue, one student's work was brought to standard, and the other student showed that he had internalized what had been taught and could explain it to his friend. The students worked the process out, and the teacher served as encourager. (I have not used the students' real names to protect their privacy, but this is their work.)

ALL ABOUT MY LIFE WEBSITE
Reading Journal #14: 02/16/2012 — "Roar"

Jeffrey

Dear Ms. H,

I am reading the book "roar". Roar is awesome, my kind of book which is action and mysterious/anomusys. It is about twins who share a strong bond between each other. I am not in red maple but I plan to join after one test book I read to see if I can achive or not so il try.

Nick (in response to Jeffrey's note)

Dear Jeffrey,

How are you doing? I like your website but I think that you could of put much more effort into it. I think that your website needs more pages and since you are a fan of basket ball you could explore my site. My site had a lot of cool stuff about basketball!

The Red Maple Awards reading program is coordinated by the Ontario School Library Association to encourage students in Grades 7 and 8 to read for enjoyment. Current Canadian books are chosen and highlighted, and students are encouraged to go online to learn about the authors and even communicate with them via email and with other students by way of a bulletin board. If students read at least five of the chosen books, they can cast a vote on the book they like best, and the results are published and shared across the province.

Younger readers can take part in the Silver Birch (Grades 3 to 6) and Blue Spruce (K to Grade 2) programs.

I think that you could put a lot more effort into your reading journal. You have only written 3 lines! You check your grammar!

This is your reading journal:

Dear Ms. H_____, I am reading the book "roar". Roar is awesome, my kind of book which is action and mysterious/anomusys. It is about twins who share a strong bond between each other. I am not in red maple but I plan to join after one test book I read to see if I can achive or not so il try.

1. You have to write Dear Nick,
2. Press space and put question number one
3. Press space again and answer the question
4. Press space again and put question number two
5. Press space again and answer the question
6. Press space again and put the question
7. Press space again and answer the question
8. Press space three times and write sincerely, Jeffrey
9. You should put A LOT more information!
10. Meet the expectations!

This says right in front of the reading journal page:
Reading Journal Weekly Expectations

- It should be in letter format.
- It needs to be a post on your website.
- All entries need to be submitted by Friday night at midnight.
- Please split your writing up into appropriate paragraphs.
- **Don't forget to put any book title in quotations.

Ms. H is the one who wrote that and if you don't do that you will get homework club.

This is how your reading journal should look like:

Dear Nick,

1. What book are you reading right now? Tell us a little bit about your book without giving anything away!

Roar is awesome, my kind of book which is action and mysterious/anomusys. It is about to twins who share a strong bond between each other.

Check your spelling for anonymous!

This is only one sentence and you need a lot more information then this!

2. Are you taking part in the Red Maple Reading Program? Why or why not? If yes, how many books have you read from it? Would you recommend them? If no, what is your reasoning?

I am not in red maple but I will plan to join after one test book? I read to see if I can achive or not so il try.

To me the sentence you wrote makes totally no sense at all!! What do you mean by test book? Capital on I !! I know Ms. H would hate that! achieve!!!! spelling check!

3.   Make another inference from your book. Flag one page, tell us what page it is, then explain using clues from the text and your own ideas why you infer that.

YOU DID NOT EVEN DO THIS QUESTION!

We did so many group works on this and you should know what an inference is now! So just before I wrap it up I think that you should re-do this whole entire reading journal again and by February 17. Please do whatever I have told you and if you still need help then comment on my website saying what you need help on! I have worked really hard on this letter that I have wrote to you!

Sincerely,
Nick

Dear Jeffrey,
One last thing to say: Can you find the errors in my response?"

Jeffrey (in response to Nick) (02/16/2012)

1.   What book are you reading right now? Tell us a little about your book, without giving anything away!

Dear Nick,

I am reading the book "Roar". Roar is awesome, my kind of book which is action and mysterious/anonymous. It is about twins who share a strong bond between each other. It is also about a unique way of something that is a problem with animals that animals are cruel and viscous to humans and that there is no point of animals. Mal Gorman the evil scientist is a kidnapper who has a special job including kids so he helps them by training and other talents for evil, but Ellie has managed to escape and her twin brother Mika has a feeling that Ellie may not be dead even though all the relatives and friends say she is he has a strong bond for her.

2.   Are you taking part in the Red Maple Reading Program? Why or why not? If yes, how many books have you read from it? Would you recommend them? If no, what is your reasoning?

I am not in the Red Maple program. I am going to ask Ms H about starting it, and also I am going to read a test book which I think will be "half brother" so I will see how hard the Red Maple program is. I hope it's on my level of reading because all the students reading in the program seem to have fun. I have tried reading in the Red Maple program but I abandoned it.

3. *Make another inference from your book.*

Inference:

I can infer that the pain Ellie is having is the pain that Mika is having. I think that because Mika and Ellie have a strong bond so they probably feel the same pain. The pain could be from Ellie getting shot down and falling in water which could have stopped her and his breathing (Ellie and Mika). Ellie could have been so hurt and since they were very close to each other the bond got even stronger. Mika has been feeling the bond ever since she supposedly died and that seems suspicious to Mika because he still feels the bond of his twin sister.

This is a really good story to make connections and is a fascinating story. I suggest you read it.

Sincerely,
Jeffrey

Nick, please give me your website address.

Ms. H [teacher]

Great work boys! Nick, you gave wonderful constructive advice to Jeffrey about his response.

Jeffrey, thank-you for listening and reading Nick's advice and then going back in and fixing it!

What wonderful self-regulation on both your parts!

This is only one example of what happens daily on a digital interface in Ms. Hubbard's Grade 7 classroom. Descriptive feedback from peers is given and taken in a positive manner, and helps to improve work. The teacher acts as an encourager and provides descriptive feedback when needed. She supports independence and understands that writing is tied to editing. Engagement in her class is high.

Final Thoughts

An Invitation

I want to know how you are putting some of these ideas into practice and would love to hear from you through my Rogers email account: doreenrose@rogers.com. Through technology, we will be able to celebrate your successes and solve any "problems of practice" together, while helping to nurture students as critical thinkers and inquiring collaborators, and as young people who love words, use them effectively, and spell them correctly when spelling matters.

For students to become successful spellers, it is necessary for us to strike a balance between their inquiries into word patterns and their growing word knowledge. Key to this balance is that information from investigations and word knowledge is cognitively stored, easily and often accessed, and directly applied to proofreading and editing. By teaching spelling through inquiry and through having students pay attention to how words work, we can enable our students to become proficent spellers and engaged problem solvers with words.

Acknowledgments

I would like to acknowledge the following people who helped in the making of this book:

- my daughter Morna, who read and reread the manuscript, offered creative ideas, and who continues to share my love of words
- Kate Revington, who worked with me patiently to edit this book, and whose advice was stellar
- Mary Macchiusi, who, as publisher, provided great encouragement and support
- the amazing principal, Deb Pratt, and staff of Treeline Public School in Peel District School Board, who welcomed me into their classrooms and allowed me to try out the practicality of ideas in this book with their students
- the students I have taught and worked with over the years, especially those who contributed helpful writing examples to Chapter 1
- and my friends, always in my corner throughout the writing process

Short Vowels: Sound Pattern

Read each word below. Listen for the vowel sound.
Sort the words in the column where they match the *sound*, not the letter.

inch, catch, does, quit, buzz
rock, last, gone, red, picnic
much, was, swam, plant, splash
guess, sticky, tall, caught, rest

sound /a/ as in class	sound /e/ as in step	sound /i/ as in tick	sound /o/ as in stop	sound /u/ as in dust

What do you notice about the spelling of the sound /u/ in *dust* and *does*?

_____

_____

_____

_____

Which words from this list would you add to your Words to Remember list?

_____

_____

_____

_____

Pembroke Publishers © 2013 *When Spelling Matters* by Doreen Scott-Dunne. ISBN 978-1-55138-277-7

Creating Lists: Long Vowels and Vowel Combinations

Create word lists with the same vowel sound and same spelling pattern as the vowels in the three columns below. The words can rhyme, but they do not always need to. For example, *take* and *taken* could go under *lake*; *rain* could go under *fair*.

lake	play	fair

When you look at your lists, think about using Notice-Wonder-Question as a way to observe and think about the words.

NOTICE — I noticed that _____

_____

WONDER — I wonder_____

_____

QUESTION — My question is _____

_____

Always remember that spelling is a thinking activity.

Pembroke Publishers © 2013 *When Spelling Matters* by Doreen Scott-Dunne. ISBN 978-1-55138-277-7

Long Vowels: Sound Pattern

Sort each word listed below into the column where it matches the visual pattern and vowel sound. For example, *played* and *day* match, but *light* and *site* do not.

say, care, great, always
seat, fair, said, main
hair, chairs, reed, tray
meat, need, kayak, seat
deed, peak, may, feed

Long /a/ as in *day*	Long /a/ as in *rain*	Long /e/ as in *eat*	Long /e/ as in *seed*	Words that don't match

What did you notice as you sorted these words?

NOTICE — I noticed that _____

_____

QUESTION — My question is _____

_____

Pembroke Publishers © 2013 *When Spelling Matters* by Doreen Scott-Dunne. ISBN 978-1-55138-277-7

One Way to Play with Words and Phrases

Try to relate color with action when creating sentences. Here are some examples for you to consider:

Red is a fire engine, speeding to the rescue.
Brown is a dry leaf, falling to the ground.

Now you make up some:

Blue is a _____ , _____ .

Black is a _____ , _____ .

Pink is a _____ , _____ .

Grey is a _____ , _____ .

Now try to involve the senses when creating sentences about color. Four prompts are provided, but first, consider these examples:

Brown is the *sound* of pine cones bursting.
Grey is the *sound* of dolphins talking.

Blue is _____ .

Green is _____ .

Purple is _____ .

Red is _____ .

Pembroke Publishers © 2013 *When Spelling Matters* by Doreen Scott-Dunne. ISBN 978-1-55138-277-7

Exploring Adjectives

Good writers may list basic adjectives and then add synonyms as they find them in their reading. See if you can add synonyms to the list below. What other basic words might you work from to develop a list?

big	large, huge, enormous, gigantic
little	
hot	
cold	
loud	
soft	

When writing, you sometimes have to describe a character. At these times, you would benefit if you could draw on a wide array of words to give your reader an idea of how the character looks, thinks, and feels. To prepare, you may want to start a list of character traits — some positive, some negative — for reference. You can add to the list over time.

Positive Character Trait	Negative Character Trait
helpful	mean
caring	selfish

Pembroke Publishers © 2013 *When Spelling Matters* by Doreen Scott-Dunne. ISBN 978-1-55138-277-7

Index